My Jesus, Your JESUS

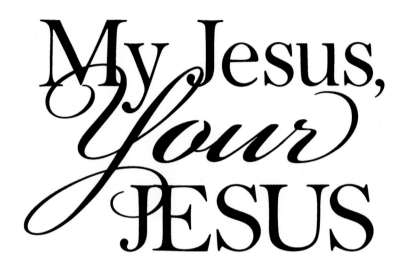

My Jesus, Your Jesus

Inspirational Messages of HOPE and HEALING

DR. BEVERLY ROSE

CREATION HOUSE

MY JESUS, YOUR JESUS: INSPIRATIONAL MESSAGES OF HOPE AND HEALING by Dr. Beverly Rose
Published by Creation House
A Charisma Media Company
600 Rinehart Road, Lake Mary, Florida 32746
www.charismamedia.com

Unless otherwise noted, all Scripture quotations are from the Holy Bible, New International Version. Copyright © 1973, 1978, 1984, 2010, 2011, International Bible Society. Used by permission.

Scripture quotations marked KJV are from the King James Version of the Bible.

Scripture quotations marked ESV are from the Holy Bible, English Standard Version, copyright © 2001 by Crossway Bibles, a division of Good News Publisher. Used by permission.

Scripture quotations marked NLT are from the Holy Bible, New Living Translation, copyright © 1996. Used by permission of Tyndale House Publishers, Inc., Wheaton, IL 60189. All rights reserved.

Scripture quotations marked NKJV are from the New King James Version of the Bible. Copyright © 1979, 1980, 1982 by Thomas Nelson, Inc., publishers. Used by permission.

Design Director: Justin Evans
Cover design by Rachel Lopez

Visit the author's website: www.docbeverlyrose.com and her Facebook page at www.facebook.com/DrBeverlyRose

Library of Congress Cataloging-in-Publication Data: 2016933814

International Standard Book Number: 978-1-62998-527-5

E-book International Standard Book Number: 978-1-62998-528-2

While the author has made every effort to provide accurate telephone numbers and Internet addresses at the time of publication, neither the publisher nor the author assumes any responsibility for errors or for changes that occur after publication.

16 17 18 19 20— 9 8 7 6 5 4 3 2

Printed in the United States of America

*This book is dedicated to Nancy W. Johnson,
a cherished friend who brings blessing
and grace to my life every day.*

CONTENTS

Contents

PROLOGUE

IMAGINE A PLACE far above your troubles. A place of hope, joy, and healing. A place where promises really do come true. An eye of the storm. Where the winds are light, the sky is blue, and the sun is bright. A spiritual sweet spot of life. Where the veil between this world and the next is so thin that you can almost touch the very hand of God.

I've been to this miraculous place, not just once but many times. Where I've been lifted above my suffering, above my despair, and above my trials. Miraculously healed from my neuromuscular disease, if only for the moment. That's because I'm healed in moments, although I've yet to be cured.

You too can discover this place when you come to know the one person who can take you there. The person who loved you first and keeps loving you to the last. Who believes in you, never leaves you, and gives you hope and a future.

Where can you find Him? You needn't search far. He's already found you. He's in your joy, your suffering, and your trials. He's deep within your heart. You need only have eyes to see and ears to hear who's already there.

So come along. Find blessedness in brokenness. Experience healing when you're hurting. Discover the peace that transcends all understanding. You can change your life for good— forever. When you make Jesus *your* Jesus.

INTRODUCTION

*I*T WAS JUST an ordinary morning this side of the other side. I gazed at the brilliant Colorado sunrise. The Front Range of the Rockies sparkled in a rosy glow. It was a captivating sight, especially for a captive like me. I shifted in my wheelchair and adjusted the thick foam pad. Out of the corner of my eye, I saw a magpie perched on a low branch of the aspen tree outside my window. It was chattering happily. *It's amazing how birds get up in the morning without complaint,* I mused. *If I were a bird, my first thought would be what a lousy night I had. I'm shivering from the cold, my feathers are dripping from the rain. And I must fix that twig that keeps sticking me in the wrong place.*

I stared at the blank computer screen. I knew I should start writing my devotional book, but I didn't know where to begin. How could I explain how meeting Jesus had changed my life? In one miraculous moment, I had gone from no life to new life. From insurmountable limitations to unlimited potential. From incapacity to empowerment. From victim to victor. All from the confines of a wheelchair, while battling a progressive neuromuscular disease.

The sun's rays filtered through the blinds. Streaks of orange splashed across my bare white walls. My mind flashed back to a different time and place. Where rays of morning light streamed through stained glass windows, bathing the pews of the old eighteenth century church. I could see myself standing at the pulpit, leaning on my crutches. Trying to conceal my shaky hands, taking deep breaths, and daring myself to speak.

Good morning. Today is the greatest day of my life. And I'm so grateful that I'm here to share it with you. Why is this day so special? Did I just win the lottery? No. Am I being honored with an award? No. Am I getting married today? No. But I'll entertain all offers after the service.

I smiled, remembering the audience's laughter in the midst of such solemnity. *I can never resist telling a good joke*, I mused, *even in a sanctuary.* I refocused on the unlikely scene.

The reason today is the greatest day of my life is because the Lord lifted me out of a sickbed so that I could come before you to attest to the truth and boundless love of Jesus Christ.

I wiped the perspiration from my forehead. Seventeen years had passed since I gave my testimony. Yet I could still feel my anxiety rising as three hundred pairs of eyes in the sanctuary stared at me. Except for the guy in the plaid suit who was sleeping in the back pew. I rubbed my aching body as my mind continued to drift back in time.

Since many of you don't know me, I'd like to tell you a little about myself. I had quite a number of accomplishments before falling ill many years ago. I earned a doctorate in clinical psychology. I held an academic appointment at Harvard Medical School. I owned a beautiful condo on a New England lake. I was only months away from earning a six-figure income as an associate director of a regional nursing home program. I thought I had it all. What I didn't know was that I was about to be stricken with a rare genetic neuromuscular disease at the height of my career—which would change everything. I was forced to resign my position, sell my condo, and move in with my parents in Florida. Two-and-a-half months later, my mother unexpectedly died. I had lost it all. I was only thirty-four years old.

I wiped a tear from my eye and stared out the window. A mountain bluebird swooped down and perched on the aspen tree, displacing the chattering magpie. His iridescent wings shimmered in the morning sunlight. Suddenly he took wing and soared high into the sky. I marveled at how the beautiful creature could fly so effortlessly without falling. *He doesn't know what it's like to suddenly plummet to the ground after reaching great heights,* I mused. I could almost hear my mother sighing, as she uttered her favorite expression, "Man plans and God laughs." *If she only knew just how prophetic her words were,* I thought. My mind flashed back in time, returning to that fateful day.

When you lose the seemingly most important things in life—money, prestige, profession, and especially a loving mother—and are left to suffer the ravages of a devastating illness, you cry out for answers. *What kind of a God would leave me to suffer like this?* I agonized. I felt desperately alone, was in terrible despair, and believed my life no longer had any purpose or meaning. But please don't weep for me. For, years later, in the confines of that very sickbed where I cried and railed against God and life, the amazing Answer came to me.

I felt a cramp in my right leg. I reached down and vigorously rubbed my calf muscle, trying to ease the pain. Life in the twenty-first century was proceeding as usual. Unlike the life-shattering events taking place inside my head, where it was still 1998. I escaped back into the past.

Then I took the one action that would change my life forever. I did the one thing I thought I would never do. I picked up a book and read about Jesus Christ. As I put the book down, I began to meditate. And, for some reason, I whispered His name. Suddenly an awesome, loving presence came over me. He was more real than any reality I had ever experienced. Truer than any truth I had ever known. God had finally revealed Himself to me in the last place on Earth I ever would have expected. My Savior had come to give me hope and a future![1]

I reached for a tissue, wiped the tears from my face, and stared out the window at the majestic Colorado landscape. I had come a long way since that day of my testimony in a small church near Boston. And an even longer way since the incredible moment I met Jesus Christ. Yet, as remarkable as that meeting had been, the miracles that soon followed had been even more amazing. Jesus had repeatedly come to my rescue, lifting me above my circumstances to a new life of hope and purpose. He had revealed to me a God like no other. A God of unconditional love, boundless caring, unfailing faithfulness, and impeccable guidance. A God who loved me too much to leave me and would be with me for all eternity. This amazing God even gave me glimpses of heaven in His healing presence.

My eyes returned to the blank computer screen. *If only people who are hurting could come to know Jesus as I know Him*, I thought. *If only they could find what I've found in Him. And discover for themselves that, despite their challenges, obstacles, disappointments, and losses, there's a powerful way to overcome in Jesus.*

Suddenly I felt a prompting in my heart. A rush of thoughts flooded my mind. Jesus was making a way for me to begin my book. The words came faster than I could type them—messages of hope, healing, and encouragement.

I stopped typing, wiped a tear from my cheek, and bowed my head in prayer.

Lord Jesus, thank You for the task You have set before me. May I honor and glorify You in the pages of this devotional. And lead those who are hurting into Your loving, healing presence. In Your precious name, amen.

The MESSAGES

He performs wonders that cannot be fathomed,
miracles that cannot be counted.

—JOB 9:10

JESUS IS MY RAINBOW OF PROMISE

I will bring you safely through the storm.

—JESUS

*G*OING THROUGH A major crisis can feel like being caught in a massive thunderstorm. The skies darken, winds kick up, hail pounds, rains flood, thunder booms, and lightning strikes. Just when you think all is lost, the winds still, the rain stops, and an arc appears in the sky. Brilliant colors of pink, purple, yellow, and orange turn the steel gray canvas into a dazzling display. The rainbow doesn't last for long. Yet it leaves a lasting impression and an enduring promise.

Noah knew the feeling. He tossed around in his wooden ark on heavy seas in wind-driven rain for over a year, while every living thing on Earth was being destroyed. After he finally set foot on dry land, he saw God's colorful sign: a magnificent rainbow that signified God's covenant of grace.

When I'm going through hard times, I think of Noah's rainbow. Just as Noah knew that God would be with him in raging storms, so do I. Just as Noah landed on solid ground, so will I. I believe in rainbows because I believe in God's promises.

Lord Jesus, we thank You for bringing us safely through the storms of our lives. When we're battered by fierce winds and pounding rains, help us cling tightly to Your promises. And to remember Noah's rainbow and Your everlasting covenant with all humanity. In Your precious name, amen.

~ɔ⊙ℓ~

Whenever the rainbow appears in the clouds, I will see
it and remember the everlasting covenant between God
and all living creatures of every kind on the earth.

—GENESIS 9:16

FOR PRAYERFUL REFLECTION

How do you hold onto the Lord's promises in the midst of the
storms in your life?

_____

_____

_____

JESUS IS MY LIGHT

I am the light in the darkness.

—JESUS

*W*HEN YOU LOOK around, you may be tempted to despair. The world is full of suffering, sin, and brokenness. You may be going through difficult trials in your life right now that are causing you to lose hope. Yet, if you look closely, you may see something extraordinary. Light breaking through the darkness. Sunshine bursting through the clouds. The very light of God breaking into your life, meeting despair with grace.

God can heal you in your suffering. He can make you whole in your brokenness. He can fill you with peace in the midst of your anxiety. He can love you when you're unlovable. Forgive you when you think you've done the unforgivable. Grant you eternity despite your mortality.

Two thousand years ago, despair met grace on the cross when Jesus gave Himself for you, saving you from your sins. He offered Himself as a living sacrifice so that you could overcome in Him, just as He overcame for you.

Let despair meet grace in your life. It's free and unmerited. Paid for with the blood, sweat, and tears of our Lord and Savior Jesus Christ—just for you.

Lord Jesus, we thank You for the light You shine into our lives. Help us to grow in Your grace. Heal us, make us whole, and transform our lives in miraculous ways. In Your precious name, amen.

_)0l_

Out of his fullness we have all received
grace in place of grace already given.
—JOHN 1:16

FOR PRAYERFUL REFLECTION

How does despair meet grace in your life?

_____

_____

_____

JESUS IS MY CONTENTMENT

Rest easy in Me.

—JESUS

IT'S NOT EASY to find contentment in life. Pressing responsibilities, commitments, and deadlines can make you feel anxious, burdened, and stressed out. Where can you find blessed relief? The apostle Paul had the answer.

Paul faced far more stress on a daily basis than most of us ever will. He endured persecution, torture, and imprisonment for many years. But he was still led to write, "I have learned the secret of being content in any and every situation, whether well fed or hungry, whether living in plenty or in want. I can do all this through him who gives me strength" (Phil. 4:12–13). Paul found his contentment in Jesus—and so can you.

Jesus knew the toxic effects of stress long before researchers discovered them. So, in love and grace, He gave you the most powerful antidote in the world—Himself.

Lay your burdens at the feet of Jesus, and you'll find blessed relief. Cast your worries upon Him, and you'll find peace and contentment. When you're feeling stressed, don't stress out. Seek out Jesus. You can rest easy in Him.

Lord Jesus, we thank You for being our remedy for stress. Help us to reach out to You to find the blessed contentment we crave. In Your precious name, amen.

꧁ꙮꙮ꧂

Come to me, all you who are weary and
burdened, and I will give you rest.
—MATTHEW 11:28

For Prayerful Reflection

In what ways does Jesus alleviate stress in your life?

_____

_____

_____

4
JESUS IS MY TRAIL GUIDE

I will lead you up steep mountains into green valleys.

—**JESUS**

O YOU CLIMB mountains? I do. Not just once in a while but every day. The mountains I climb are not made of clay. They're made from the pain, disappointments, and challenges in life. Yet overcoming them is like climbing real mountains. It takes determination and a willingness to persevere without falling into despair. To push through without giving up. To be mentally tough, calm, cool, and collected. And to think clearly without panicking.

Yet I still couldn't climb one inch without my backpack full of climbing equipment—not from REI but from God. A backpack filled with scripture, prayer, and fellowship. These essential tools help me to faithfully follow my expert guide. Who's not a Sherpa but the Good Shepherd, guiding me safely along the way—all the way to the top.

Lord Jesus, we thank You that You guide us through our many trials. Enable us to utilize the spiritual tools You give us. Help us to follow Your lead, as we climb the steep mountains of our lives. In Your precious name, amen.

My sheep listen to my voice; I know them, and they follow me. I give them eternal life, and they shall never perish; no one will snatch them out of my hand.
—JOHN 10:27–28

For Prayerful Reflection

How do you make it through your trials by following Jesus's lead?

_____

_____

_____

JESUS IS MY STRENGTH

I will empower you when you are weak.

—JESUS

*L*IFE'S TRIALS CAN wear you down and sap you of your strength. When you're feeling weak, discouraged, and unable to cope, where can you turn?

Every day I face seemingly impossible obstacles from the confines of this wheelchair. I wake up in the morning exhausted, wondering how I will ever get through another day. Yet I rise. Not under my own power, but by the power of Jesus Christ. Thankfully, I don't have to rely on my own strength to get me through the day—and neither do you.

Paul wrote: "For when I am weak, then I am strong" (2 Cor. 12:10). At first glance, this seems to be an impossibility. How can you be both strong and weak at the same time? The answer is you can—if you have the power of Jesus Christ within you.

In our world, people boast about their strength. But, like Paul, you can boast about your weakness. Every time you are strong when you are weak. Every time you accomplish the seemingly impossible in Jesus, you show the world the enormity of His power, mercy, and grace.

When you feel weak and discouraged, let the Lord empower you. You'll see for yourself how strong you can be when you are weak.

Lord Jesus, we thank You that You give us strength when we are weak. Help us to call out to You in our weakness. Empower us to accomplish the seemingly impossible in You. In Your precious name, amen.

~ﬆﬆ~

But he said to me, "My grace is sufficient for you, for
my power is made perfect in weakness." Therefore I
will boast all the more gladly about my weaknesses,
so that Christ's power may rest on me.

—2 CORINTHIANS 12:9

FOR PRAYERFUL REFLECTION

How do you find strength in Jesus to overcome challenges in
your life?

_____

_____

_____

6

JESUS IS MY HOPE

I answer your hope with My promises.

—JESUS

*T*HERE'S A DIFFERENCE between having hope and having Christian hope. If you have a desire for something to come true, you have hope. But Christian hope is far more. Before I became a Christian, I had so many hopes. I hoped I would meet the perfect guy, get married, raise children, and have a successful career. I knew my hopes wouldn't necessarily all come true. I realized that the desires of my heart might go no further than the confines of my heart. But I hoped anyway— until I lost all hope. That's when I discovered Christian hope— and I never lost hope again.

Christian hope is not just a desire, a want, or a feeling. It's a confident expectation and a certainty about God's promises. Christian hope is being so convinced of the truth that you take God at His Word. It's knowing that you're forgiven, saved, and have eternal life. It's believing that God will always work to bring about good for those who love Him. Christian hope is solely, simply knowing Jesus Christ!

Lord Jesus, we thank You for the hope we have in You. Help us to not base our hopes on our wants and desires, but on the solid certainty of Your promises. May we always place our hope in You and in You alone. In Your precious name, amen.

Now faith is confidence in what we hope for
and assurance about what we do not see.
—HEBREWS 11:1

FOR PRAYERFUL REFLECTION

How does having Christian hope change the way you live your life?

_____

_____

_____

JESUS IS MY PRAYER POWER

Your prayers are pleasing to Me.

—**JESUS**

*S*OME PEOPLE BELIEVE that to make their prayers powerful, they must choose the right words. Or fall to their knees. Or pray in church. Or have their pastor pray for them. When I was a child, I would kneel beside my bed and pray. I was convinced that being on my knees and saying just the right words would ensure that my prayers would reach God. When I could no longer kneel, I wondered just how powerful my prayers could possibly be. Thankfully, I know now that the Lord hears me just as well from my wheelchair, even when my words are far from perfect.

Prayer is powerful not because of how you say it, where you say it, or the person who says it for you. Prayer is powerful because the prayers of a righteous person are pleasing to God. The good news is that this includes you! Jesus made you righteous when He died for your sins on the cross, so that you could stand blameless before God in prayer.

So pray your prayers with a humble heart. Seek the Lord's will in all things. The Lord will listen intently to your prayers. He'll become a partner in your problems—and always give you His best answer.

Lord Jesus, we thank You that our prayers are pleasing to You. Help us to come to prayer with a righteous and humble heart. Trusting that You will give us Your best answer in Your perfect timing. In Your precious name, amen.

The prayer of a righteous person is powerful and effective.
—JAMES 5:16

For Prayerful Reflection

What makes your prayers powerful?

_____

_____

_____

8
JESUS IS MY LIFEGUARD

I will rescue you.

—JESUS

*S*OMETIMES THE CURRENTS of life can be so strong that they threaten to pull you under. Where can you find rescue when you're drowning? Look to the shore. You won't see a sign that says: "Swim at your own risk. No lifeguard on duty." Instead you'll see Someone sitting high on the lifeguard tower, watching out for you. Ready to rescue you the moment you start going under. To hold you up when you're going down and stop you from sinking. He'll pull you to shore and save your life. Just as He rescued you from sin and death two thousand years ago. When you have Jesus Christ, your eternal lifeguard, you never have to swim at your own risk.

Lord Jesus, we thank You that You are our rescuer. Help us to call out to You when we're going under. Lift us up and bring us safely to shore. In Your precious name, amen.

Then they cried out to the LORD in their trouble,
and he delivered them from their distress.
—PSALM 107:6

FOR PRAYERFUL REFLECTION

In what ways does the Lord rescue you?

_____

_____

_____

9

JESUS IS MY VISION

See life through Me.

—JESUS

*F*OR ONE MIRACULOUS moment, I stood atop a mountain. Below me were puffy white clouds. Above me was a sparkling blue sky. In that brilliant landscape of jagged mountain peaks and stands of golden aspen, I saw God. Not because He was visible, but because I had vision.

Helen Keller said, "The only thing worse than being blind is having sight but no vision."[1] Having vision in the Lord means seeing what others don't see. Having faith in what others refuse to believe. Doing what others deem impossible. Having vision in the Lord means living your life according to God's will, not your own. Finding your purpose in Him. Doing mighty works in His name that change the lives of others, as well as your own. Having vision in the Lord brings meaning and blessing to your life beyond anything in this world. You don't have to stand on a mountaintop to see God. All you need is vision!

Lord Jesus, we thank You that believing is seeing. Help us to have vision to see You all around us and within us. Enable us to see our lives through You. In Your precious name, amen.

Then Jesus told him, "Because you have seen me, you have believed; blessed are those who have not seen and yet have believed."
—JOHN 20:29

For Prayerful Reflection

What does having vision in the Lord enable you to see?

_____

_____

_____

10

JESUS IS MY REASON FOR BEING

I'm the reason you were born.

—JESUS

DO YOU EVER wonder why you were born? You're not alone. A wise person once said, "The two most important days in your life are the day you are born and the day you find out why."[1] I would add a third day—the day I was born again. Because, on that glorious day, I truly found out why I was born.

When you're in Christ, you don't have to struggle with the question of why you were born. You already know. You were born because He loves you and longs for relationship with you. You were born to love Him and others as yourself. To serve Him and to serve others. To be salt and light in a fallen world. Other people may struggle to find meaning in their lives. But Jesus infuses your life with meaning because you mean so very much to Him.

Lord Jesus, we thank You that You are the meaning in our lives. Help us to discern Your will and to live out Your perfect purpose for our lives every day. In Your precious name, amen.

Jesus replied, "Very truly I tell you, no one can see the kingdom of God unless they are born again....Flesh gives birth to flesh, but the Spirit gives birth to spirit."
—JOHN 3:3, 6

For Prayerful Reflection

In what ways is Jesus your reason for being?

_____

_____

_____

JESUS IS MY RANSOM

I paid the price so that you could have life.

—JESUS

ACH DAY YOU live, you pay a price in the many trials you face. But Jesus faced even greater trials and paid an even higher price so that you could fully live this day. He suffered and gave His life so that you could have a new life—a life of hope, promise, meaning, purpose, grace, and forgiveness. You can honor the day Jesus gave His life for you by making each day of your life count for Him.

In my life, this means never giving up no matter how hard it gets. Proclaiming His name no matter how much the forces of evil conspire against me. Holding onto the light no matter how dark it gets.

The Lord paid the ransom so that you can have life today—and have it to the fullest. Why not honor His sacrifice by living today to the fullest in Him?

Lord Jesus, we thank You for being the light in our darkness. The meaning in our emptiness. The hope in our fallenness. Help us to use this day for good so that we can honor the price You paid for it. In Your precious name, amen.

This is how we know what love is: Jesus Christ laid down his life for us.

—1 JOHN 3:16

For Prayerful Reflection

What will you do today to honor the price Jesus paid for your life?

_____

_____

_____

12

JESUS IS MY BREATH

I am in the wind.

—JESUS

*T*HE ANCIENT HEBREWS believed that the very Spirit of God was in the wind. They had a special word, *ruach*, which meant wind, breath, or spirit. Imagine feeling so close to God that you can feel His very presence in the wind!

Living in modern society, we've lost that closeness. We live indoor lives. We're glued to computer screens, televisions, iPads, and iPhones. But you can still feel God's presence, just as the ancient Hebrews did. Just walk outside. Breathe in the air and thank God that every breath you take is by His grace. While you're there, recall a favorite Scripture verse and thank God that the Word is God-breathed. Rejoice in the beauty of life and thank God that He breathed life into you. God is so close that you can feel His breath. You need only turn your cheek to the breeze and believe!

Lord Jesus, we thank You for breathing life into us. We know that every breath we take is by Your grace. When we're longing for closeness with You, help us to seek Your presence all around us, especially in the wind. In Your precious name, amen.

Then the LORD God formed a man from the dust of
the ground and breathed into his nostrils the breath
of life, and the man became a living being.
—GENESIS 2:7

For Prayerful Reflection

In what ways do you find closeness with the Lord?

_____

_____

_____

13

JESUS IS MY FREEDOM

Abide in Me. I will set you free.

—JESUS

 o you feel trapped in your life? Do you wish you could be free? You may think that freedom means having control over your life and being the master of your own fate. If this sounds more freeing than serving the Master of the universe, you haven't met Jesus Christ.

When you're free to pursue material things, you can become a slave to your possessions. But in Jesus, you're not attached to the things of this world. When you're free to pursue instant gratification, you can become a slave to your desires. But in Jesus, you have everything you could possibly desire. When you're free to make unlimited income, you can become a slave to greed. But in Jesus, you have all the riches you could ever want. When you're free to feed your ego, you can become a slave to proving your self-worth. But in Jesus, you're already worthy. When you're free to indulge yourself, you can become a slave to sin. But in Jesus, you are forgiven. Which kind of freedom do you prefer? You're free to choose.

Lord Jesus, we thank You that You set us free. Help us to break our attachment to the things of this world and to embrace You and You alone. In Your precious name, amen.

Then you will know the truth, and the truth will set you free.
—JOHN 8:32

For Prayerful Reflection

In what ways does the Lord set you free?

_____

_____

_____

14

JESUS IS MY REASON TO REJOICE

I will make you glad.

—JESUS

*T*HE BIBLE TELLS us that the Lord made this day, so we should rejoice and be glad. But what if you don't have much to be joyful about today? Maybe you're in pain, grieving, or miserable at work. Maybe you're having financial problems or your children are in trouble. It's not always easy to wake up in the morning and rejoice and be glad.

Sometimes my muscles are so painful and I'm so exhausted that it's hard to embrace the day. That's when I am reminded that when things aren't looking up, the Lord is waiting to lift me up. To comfort me, strengthen me, and give me hope. To infuse my day with meaning and purpose.

When you can't embrace the day, embrace Jesus Christ. Feel His love, care, and faith in you. And suddenly, amazingly, you'll rejoice—and be glad!

Lord Jesus, we thank You that no matter our circumstances, You are always there to lift us up. Help us to call out to You when we're hurting. Embrace us with Your love and grace so that we may be glad! In Your precious name, amen.

This is the day the LORD has made; we
will rejoice and be glad in it.
—PSALM 118:24, NKJV

For Prayerful Reflection

In what ways will you rejoice in the Lord today?

_____

_____

_____

15

JESUS IS MY OVERCOMING

Overcome in Me, for I have overcome the world.

—JESUS

ESUS WARNED THAT we will have trouble in this world. That's not a very optimistic statement coming from the Prince of Peace! Yet His words have never been truer. We live in a time of war and threats of terrorism at home and abroad. There are school shootings, church shootings, and shootings on the streets of our cities. We face threats of deadly diseases, such as cancer and heart disease. How can anyone possibly cope?

You will never be able to overcome all your troubles in this world. But, just as Jesus overcame the world, He empowers you to overcome in Him. Just as He rose from the grave, He enables you to rise above your circumstances and find your answers in Him. When you overcome in Jesus, you not only transform your own life. You also become a living testimony, transforming the lives of others in amazing ways.

Life in this fallen world may seem like a losing battle. But call upon Jesus. You'll discover that in Him you have already won.

Lord Jesus, we thank You that just as You overcame the world, You enable us to overcome in You. Help us to face our fears, doubts, helplessness, and despair, and to find our peace and victory in You. In Your precious name, amen.

I have told you these things, so that in me you may
have peace. In this world you will have trouble.
But take heart! I have overcome the world.

—JOHN 16:33

For Prayerful Reflection

In what ways does Jesus help you overcome your trials in life?

_____

_____

_____

16

JESUS IS MY WELCOME GUEST

Invite Me into your heart, and I will bless you.

—JESUS

*T*HESE DAYS, INTERIOR design is big business. People pay plenty of money to have their homes staged so that prospective buyers will be eager to move in.

When I invited the Lord to make His home in me, I was worried. No matter how much I cleaned up my act, I could never be a fitting abode for Him. No amount of interior decorating could bring me up to His standards. *Why would He want to go "slumming" in my heart?* I wondered. I needn't have worried.

When the Lord comes to abide in us, He takes us as we are. He delights when we clean ourselves up. But He doesn't stand outside the door waiting for us to finish the job. He comes right in and roughs it right along with us.

When you open your heart to the Lord, you needn't fear His rejection of your invitation. He will not take a white glove and inspect every nook and cranny before entering. He will not turn His nose up at your décor. The Lord wants to make His home in you no matter how dingy your interior design. Now that's amazing grace!

Lord Jesus, we thank You for making Your home in us. Help us to faithfully and lovingly honor Your presence in our hearts. Enable us to be more gracious hosts by striving to become more like You every day. In Your precious name, amen.

_ஹ_

Then Christ will make his home in your
hearts as you trust in him.
—EPHESIANS 3:17, NLT

FOR PRAYERFUL REFLECTION

How are you cleaning up your act to honor the Lord's presence in your heart?

_____

_____

_____

17

JESUS IS MY HEALER

I make a way for you to heal.

—JESUS

DO YOU WONDER if God can really heal you? When Jesus walked the earth, He performed many healings. He cured people with a multitude of afflictions, such as blindness, leprosy, epilepsy, and paralysis. But does Jesus still perform healings? Can you be miraculously healed today?

For years I've prayed to the Lord for healing, but I haven't been cured. I continue to pray that I will be physically healed by the Lord's hand. Or someday cured by a physician utilizing gene therapy, guided by the Lord's hand. Yet I find healing in so many other ways. I feel physically healed in those moments when I experience the palpable loving presence of Jesus. I find spiritual healing when I'm serving the Lord and ministering to others. I find emotional healing when I experience the joy of those who also find hope and promise in Jesus.

Healing comes in many forms through the love and grace of Jesus Christ. Jesus has the desire, grace, and power to heal you. If you're praying for healing, you can rest assured that God's healing hand is always at work in your life. Healing you in ways too numerous to count!

Lord Jesus, we thank You for healing us in countless ways. Help us to believe in Your love, power, and desire to heal us. Enable us to reach out to You when we're hurting and in need of healing. In Your precious name, amen.

~oОe~

Praise the LORD, my soul, and forget not all his
benefits—who forgives all your sins and heals all
your diseases, who redeems your life from the pit
and crowns you with love and compassion.
—PSALM 103:2–4

FOR PRAYERFUL REFLECTION

In what ways does the Lord heal you?

_____

_____

_____

18

JESUS IS MY EYES OF FAITH

I give you eyes to see.

—JESUS

HAVE YOU DISCOVERED your eyes of faith? They're often found when your other pair of eyes fail. When you lose sight of hope. When you want to see the Lord, but can't. When you want to see Him working in your life, but don't.

The Lord knew that you would have hard times in life. That's why He gave you two pairs of eyes: one pair to see the world and the other pair to see by faith. Your eyes of faith don't need to see to believe; they believe to see. They see light in the darkness and God when He seems to be absent. They envision hope and a future when your dreams are dashed. They see your life in a whole new light.

When you're going through hard times, use your eyes of faith. You'll discover that two pairs of eyes are far better than one.

Lord Jesus, we thank You for giving us eyes of faith. Help us to use them to behold light in the midst of darkness, hope in the midst of despair, and Your loving presence in the midst of trials. In Your precious name, amen.

For we live by faith, not by sight.
—2 CORINTHIANS 5:7

FOR PRAYERFUL REFLECTION

What do your eyes of faith see?

_____

_____

_____

19

JESUS IS MY CONFIDANT

You can trust Me to understand.

—JESUS

*D*O YOU FEEL like people just don't understand what you're going through? They may try to be supportive. They may sympathize and reassure you. They may attempt to convince you that everything will be all right. But in your heart you know that they can't possibly understand.

If you're looking for someone who truly understands, look to the Person who knows you better than you know yourself. Who won't placate you, patronize you, or humor you. Who sees the truth of your situation and will always tell you the truth because He *is* the truth. Who knows your heart because He resides there.

Jesus understands what you're going through because of the many trials He faced on Earth. Ridicule, betrayal, beatings, desertion, temptation, and crucifixion. If anyone knows what it's like to experience hardship, it's the Lord. If anyone can understand, it's Jesus. Call out to Him. You'll never feel more understood.

Lord Jesus, we thank You for coming to Earth and becoming one of us. If anyone knows what it's like to be us, it's You. Help us to reach out to You when we need true understanding. In Your precious name, amen.

✧

Trust in him at all times, you people; pour out
your hearts to him, for God is our refuge.
—PSALM 62:8

FOR PRAYERFUL REFLECTION

What do you think Jesus understands about you that no one else can?

_____

_____

_____

20

JESUS IS MY SIGNALER

I speak into your life.

—JESUS

*J*ESUS SPEAKS INTO your life in so many ways. He sends signals to you like a signaler relaying radio and telephone messages to military personnel on the front line. Yet the messages that the Lord sends you are transmitted in far more profound and creative ways, designed especially for you. How can you detect His signals?

Jesus speaks into your life through His Word and the words He places on the lips of others that are meant for you. Through the events He arranges in your life that turn out better than those you had planned. Through the people He sends into your life who change your life forever. Through the beauty of His creation. Through radiant rainbows and remarkable healings. Jesus also speaks within you through the promptings of your heart and the still small voice in your soul.

If you want to detect the Lord's signals, open yourself up to His presence. Nurture a meaningful relationship with Him. Approach Him with humility, pureness of heart, and an obedient spirit. Empty yourself, and you'll find the Lord filling you up. Pray and listen, and you'll hear the Lord speaking into your heart, your soul, and your life in ways you never imagined possible!

Lord Jesus, we thank You that You speak into our lives in so many ways. Help us to develop eyes to see and ears to hear You in every moment of our lives. In Your precious name, amen.

~ollo~

For God does speak—now one way, now
another—though no one perceives it.
—Job 33:14

FOR PRAYERFUL REFLECTION

How does Jesus speak into your life?

_____

_____

_____

21

JESUS IS MY CONSTANT COMPANION

I am with you always.

—JESUS

SOMETIMES I WONDER why Jesus chooses to be with me in every messy moment of my life. He certainly has far better places to hang out—like in heaven. If I had a choice, I'd rather commune with angels, wouldn't you?

Yet Jesus left the comforts of heaven to come into our fallen world. Not to hang out all day in some fancy place like Solomon's Temple, surrounded by gold and silver. But in the shanties of the unwanted, the poor, and the sick. Jesus could have stayed in heaven and led from above, but He chose to go to Earth below. He could have commanded people to bow down at His feet, but He bowed down to wash theirs. Why? The answer can be summed up in one word: *love!*

You needn't doubt why Jesus chooses to be with you. It's because He loved you first and keeps loving you to the last. Just as He came to Earth two thousand years ago, He wants to be with you now—no matter what, where, or when. He's with you in every messy moment of your life because He loves you too much to wait for Sunday. Now that's amazing love!

Lord Jesus, we thank You that You are always with us. Help us to embrace Your loving presence in all the moments of our lives. In triumph and failure, happiness and despair, and joy and sorrow. In Your precious name, amen.

And surely I am with you always,
to the very end of the age.
—MATTHEW 28:20

For Prayerful Reflection

In what ways do you experience the presence of Jesus in the messy moments of your life?

_____

_____

_____

22

JESUS IS MY BEGINNING

Come begin in Me.

—**JESUS**

*W*HEN JESUS PROCLAIMED on the cross, "It is finished," it was only the beginning. Jesus finished His mission on Earth so that your life could begin in Him. He bore His suffering so that He could bear your suffering with you. He paid for your sins so that He could bring about forgiveness for you and ensure that you would have blessed peace with the Father for eternity. Jesus sacrificed Himself for you so that you could be adopted into God's family and live a brand new life in His love, protection, and care. A life not just of hope but also of promises fulfilled. When Jesus said, "It is finished," that's when it all started for you. When His day was over, a new day began for you. Will you begin each day in Him?

Lord, we thank You that You finished Your work on the cross so that You could begin a good work in us. We're grateful that when Your day was over, a new day began for us. Help us to honor Your sacrifice by living each day in You, through You, and for You. In Your precious name, amen.

When he had received the drink, Jesus said, "It is finished." With that, he bowed his head and gave up his spirit.
—JOHN 19:30

FOR PRAYERFUL REFLECTION

How can you begin each new day in Jesus?

_____

_____

_____

23

JESUS IS MY BEST ANSWER TO PRAYER

Wait upon Me. I will give you My best answer.

—JESUS

*D*O YOU EVER wonder why God doesn't promptly answer your prayers? After all, Jesus said, "Ask and it will be given to you" (Matt. 7:7). Why isn't it always immediately given to you when you ask?

When I began having troubling physical symptoms, I sought out the best medical minds in Boston. The doctors were perplexed. Test after test produced no definitive diagnosis. I prayed for an answer, but it took sixteen years to be diagnosed. The Lord finally made a way for me to reach a top researcher in the world, who diagnosed me with a rare genetic neuromuscular disease.

Prayers go unanswered all the time for various reasons. Sometimes God says no because what you ask for isn't within His will. Or it isn't for your ultimate good. Or it isn't the right time. Or perhaps there's something standing between you and God, such as unrepented sin, disobedience, pride, ego, or unwillingness to forgive. But don't despair. Work hard to discern God's perfect will for you. Pray your best prayers and don't stop praying. Be patient and trust. God *will* hear you. He'll give you His best answer in His perfect timing and bring about the perfect solution. Something that you may never have considered or imagined possible. An answer that could only have come by grace.

Lord Jesus, we thank You for giving us Your best answers to our prayers. Help us to come to You with a repentant and humble heart. To be patient, trust, and pray unceasingly. May Your will be done! In Your precious name, amen.

⁓◌◌⌐

This is the confidence we have in approaching God: that
if we ask anything according to his will, he hears us.
—1 John 5:14

For Prayerful Reflection

Reflect upon a time when you waited on the Lord for an answer
to prayer. How did the Lord's answer turn out for the best?

_____

_____

_____

24

JESUS IS MY FORGIVENESS

You are forgiven.

—JESUS

*D*o YOU FEEL guilty about things you've done in your life? You're not alone. We may ask others for forgiveness, make amends, and try to move on. But sometimes it's difficult to overcome the guilt and forgive ourselves. The Lord knew that we're sinners who inevitably fall. That's why He did something so remarkable that it resounds to this very day. Jesus gave His life so that we could be forgiven.

You can honor the sacrifice Jesus made for you by claiming the victory over sin that He won for you. Focus on His saving grace, not on your guilt. On His sacrifice, not on your shame. On His making you right before God, not on what you did wrong. Confess your mistakes to the Lord and express genuine regret and remorse. This will go a long way toward honoring your relationship with Him.

When you're feeling guilty about things you've done in the past, don't despair. You have already been forgiven. Now, all you have to do is make your wrongs right. The Lord forgives you—so why not forgive yourself?

Lord Jesus, we thank You that You paid the ultimate price for our sins, so that we could be forgiven. When we sin, help us to humbly come to You in earnest repentance. Enable us to forgive ourselves as You forgive us. In Your precious name, amen.

If we confess our sins, he is faithful and just and will forgive us our sins and purify us from all unrighteousness.
—1 JOHN 1:9

For Prayerful Reflection

How are you able to forgive yourself when you do something that you think is unforgivable?

_____

_____

_____

25

JESUS IS MY ENDURANCE

Fix your eyes on Me, and you will arrive
where you're destined to be.

—**JESUS**

*L*IFE CAN SEEM like a series of slow, almost impercep-
tible steps. Sometimes we take two steps forward and
one step back. At other times we take two steps back and one
step forward.

When I catch a virus, every symptom of my neuromuscular
disease is exacerbated as my weak immune system struggles
to defeat the germs. It can take months to recover. Meanwhile,
I see my functional capacity slipping away day by day. It feels
like I'm taking two steps back and one step forward. Yet, step
by step, by the Lord's grace, I eventually recover.

When you walk with Jesus, you can rest assured that, even
when you believe you're taking two steps back and one step
forward, the Lord is ordering your steps in the right direction.
You may not initially see what you're overcoming by your faith,
your persistence, and your trust in Him. You may not see the
finish line. But fix your eyes on Jesus and keep on going no
matter what. And you will arrive where you're destined to be.

Lord Jesus, we thank You that You always lead us in
the right direction. Enable us to persevere through
our trials and not become discouraged. Help us to
fix our eyes on You and You alone. In Your precious
name, amen.

And let us run with perseverance the race marked out for us,
fixing our eyes on Jesus, the pioneer and perfecter of faith.
—HEBREWS 12:1–2

For Prayerful Reflection

When you're going through trials, how does it help to fix your eyes on Jesus?

_____

_____

_____

26

JESUS IS MY COMPETENCE

In Me, there are no limits.

—JESUS

O YOU WISH to accomplish great things but feel limited by your circumstances? Maybe you don't feel you have the skills, money, resources, or physical stamina. Or you have fears and doubts. The next time you're stopped because of your perceived limitations, turn to Someone who knows no limits.

God is not limited by the little you think you have. Jesus fed five thousand people with only five loaves of bread. God is not limited by your lack of strength. David, a young shepherd armed with only a slingshot, slew the mighty warrior Goliath. God is not limited by your circumstances. Samson struck down a thousand men with only the jawbone of a donkey. God is not limited by your doubts. Sarah laughed when she heard God say that she would conceive a child when she was ninety years old. But she gave birth to a healthy son, Isaac. God is not limited by your fears. Peter was so scared when he saw Jesus arrested that he denied Him three times. But God used Peter as the rock upon which He built His church.

When you hold back because of the little you think you have or can do, think again. If Jesus could multiply five loaves to feed five thousand people—and still have leftovers—think of what He can bring about in your life!

Lord Jesus, we thank You that in You there are no limits. Help us not to be stopped by our perceived limitations. Enable us to march forward confidently in You, knowing that You are all we need to accomplish great things. In Your precious name, amen.

_꩜_

Not that we are competent in ourselves to claim anything
for ourselves, but our competence comes from God.

—2 CORINTHIANS 3:5

FOR PRAYERFUL REFLECTION

Recall a time when you accomplished a seemingly impossible
goal. In what ways did Jesus enable you to go beyond your
limitations to reach it?

_____

_____

_____

27

JESUS IS MY PRAYER

Pray to Me. I will give you Myself.

—JESUS

DO YOU EVER wonder why you bother to pray? If God already knows what you need before you ask, what's the point?

I've struggled with this question for a long time. Day after day I've gone to bed praying for physical healing. And day after day, I have awakened with this disease. *Why bother to pray at all?* I've wondered. *After all, the Lord must see me sitting here in this wheelchair.* Then I had a thought: *Maybe prayer is more for my sake than for God's.*

Prayer is a special time for communion with the Lord. When you can pour out your heart to Him, express your dreams and desires, and learn His perfect will for you. It's an anointed place where you can feel loved, cherished, valued, and heard. It's a time when you can acknowledge your dependence on the Lord, confess your sins, and repent. It's an opportunity to lift your voice in adoration and praise. And to thank the Lord for His mercy and grace.

The Lord may not always give you the things you ask for in prayer. What He grants you will be according to His will. But you can rest assured that He will always give you what you need most—time with Him. The best gift is not what you get out of prayer, but what you get when you're in prayer—none other than Jesus Christ Himself.

> *Lord Jesus, we thank You for the privilege of spending precious time with You in prayer. Help us to value prayer not only as a time of petition, confession, repentance, adoration, and praise. But also for the joy and privilege of communion with You! In Your precious name, amen.*

⁂

The LORD is near to all who call on him, to
all who call on him in truth.
—PSALM 145:18

FOR PRAYERFUL REFLECTION

In what ways do you benefit from prayer?

_____

_____

_____

28

JESUS IS MY TRUTH

I am more real than reality.

—**JESUS**

*I*S JESUS FOR real? It's hard to believe that Someone loves you unconditionally. Knows you better than you know yourself. Is always there for you. Died on a cross so that you could be forgiven. He sounds too good to be true.

If you ever doubt whether Jesus is real, just ask the people who know Him best. Those who walk with Him every day and pray to Him every night. They'll tell you something quite amazing. How their lives have wondrously changed. How they've been incredibly transformed. How they've found amazing joy. They'll tell you that Jesus is marvelously and miraculously 100 percent real—the absolute truth!

Lord Jesus, we thank You that You change our lives in miraculous ways. Help us to embrace the truth of Your reality and the power of Your presence. In Your precious name, amen.

Jesus answered, "I am the way and the truth and the life."
—JOHN 14:6

FOR PRAYERFUL REFLECTION

In what ways has the truth of Jesus transformed you and your life?

_____

_____

_____

29

JESUS IS MY PURPOSE

In Me, you know what you're meant to be.

—JESUS

OUTSIDE MY WINDOW stands a tall evergreen tree. I love to watch it gently sway in the breeze. Shed melting snow from its branches in winter. Cast shadows in the setting summer sun. There's something peaceful about that stately tree. It seems to know its purpose, as it gracefully fulfills its part in God's creation. Withstanding fierce winds, heavy snowstorms, and pounding hail without complaint. It's not envious of the aspens that have brilliantly colored fall leaves. Or of the cottonwoods that attract more birds in spring. It just does what evergreens are meant to do. I imagine this makes the Lord smile!

Lord Jesus, we thank You that Your creation not only brings beauty into our lives but also lessons to learn. Help us to be more like the evergreen tree. To live out our purpose with dignity and grace. To accept what you meant us to be. And to be grateful for our purpose in Your kingdom. In Your precious name, amen.

⹃⹌

But I have raised you up for this very purpose,
that I might show you my power and that my
name might be proclaimed in all the earth.
—EXODUS 9:16

FOR PRAYERFUL REFLECTION

What do you believe is your purpose in God's kingdom?

_____

_____

_____

30

JESUS IS MY REFUGE FROM FEAR

I will calm your fears with My love.

—JESUS

*I*N THIS FALLEN world, there's much to fear. Illness, job loss, financial collapse, crime, terrorism... The list is long. Yet there is one thing you need never fear. One thing you can rely on no matter what happens.

The Bible tells us, "The Lord is with me; I will not be afraid. What can mere mortals do to me?" (Ps. 118:6). The amazing fact is that Lord is always with us no matter what. You'd think this would be enough to calm our fears. Yet Jesus's own disciples cowered in fear when their boat was in danger of sinking in a raging storm. Even though Jesus was right there with them in the same boat! So what hope is there for the rest of us?

Your hope rests in God's love. Believing that His love is so strong that absolutely nothing can separate you from it. Knowing that His love is so perfect that His "perfect love drives out fear" (1 John 4:18). The Lord doesn't want you to fear the "what ifs." He wants you to trust in "what is." To have faith in the great "I Am" and His boundless love.

When you're afraid, cast your fears upon the Lord. He will calm your fears with His love, just as He calmed the waters for His beloved disciples in a raging storm. Now that's perfect love!

Lord Jesus, we thank You that we can never be separated from Your love. Help us to call out to You when we're afraid. So that You will replace our fears with Your amazing love. In Your precious name, amen.

For I am convinced that neither death nor life, neither
angels nor demons, neither the present nor the future,
nor any powers, neither height nor depth, nor anything
else in all creation, will be able to separate us from
the love of God that is in Christ Jesus our Lord.
—ROMANS 8:38–39

FOR PRAYERFUL REFLECTION

How does the love of Jesus help you to overcome your fears?

_____

_____

_____

31

JESUS IS MY ENLIGHTENMENT

I give you light by which to see.

—JESUS

SEEING LIFE IN Jesus's light is not the same as seeing life in ordinary light. In His light, everything looks different. When I see my life in the light of Jesus, I don't just see obstacles. I also see opportunities to overcome them. I don't just see trials. I also see occasions to test my faith. I don't just see death. I also see a spectacular heaven waiting for me. I don't just see my weak body in a wheelchair. I also see a vibrant soul lifted above circumstances to minister, teach, care, and love. I don't just see me. I also see the Son of God in me.

C. S. Lewis wrote, "I believe in Christianity as I believe the sun has risen, not only because I see it, but because by it I see everything else."[1] Because the Son has risen, we can see everything else by His light. Praise the Lord that He gives us light by which see!

Lord Jesus, we thank You that in Your light we can truly see. Help us to see everything in our lives by Your precious light. In Your precious name, amen.

When Jesus spoke again to the people, he said, "I am the light of the world. Whoever follows me will never walk in darkness, but will have the light of life."

—JOHN 8:12

FOR PRAYERFUL REFLECTION

What do you see when you see life by the light of Jesus?

_____

_____

_____

32

JESUS IS MY PERFECT DISCERNMENT

Seek out My perfect will for your life.

—JESUS

*I*T'S OFTEN HARD to know what God has planned for our lives. How can you discern His perfect will for you?

Get to know the Lord through a daily personal relationship with Him. Walk with Him, talk with Him, and pray to Him. The more you commune with the Lord, the more you'll become familiar with His voice and His movements. Be on the lookout for the many ways He speaks into your life. Through the promptings of the Holy Spirit, the counsel of Christian friends, and changing circumstances. Through scriptural passages that suddenly reveal a different meaning in light of your current dilemma. Remember that God's movements can be subtle. His still small voice may be barely audible. So watch and listen intently. Allow the Holy Spirit to work within you. "Do not conform to the pattern of this world, but be transformed by the renewing of your mind. Then you will be able to test and approve what God's will is—his good, pleasing and perfect will" (Rom. 12:2).

Pray unceasingly for discernment and allow God the time and space to work in your life. Don't force it. When you feel a prompting that you believe is from the Lord, follow it. If your discernment is wrong, you can rest assured that He will make it right. If a sense of peace comes over you, it's often a sign that you've accurately discerned God's will for you. Then it's time to thank the Lord for His love and grace.

Lord Jesus, we thank You that You have a perfect plan for our lives. Help us to discern Your plan and to surrender to Your perfect will. In Your precious name, amen.

Whether you turn to the right or to the left, your ears will
hear a voice behind you, saying, "This is the way; walk in it."
—ISAIAH 30:21

FOR PRAYERFUL REFLECTION

How do you discern God's will for your life?

_____

_____

_____

33

JESUS IS MY PEACE

Cast your burdens upon me, and I will give you peace.

—JESUS

IN OUR SOCIETY, there's much to be anxious about. Keeping your job, a roof over your head, and food on the table. Maintaining your health and keeping your loved ones healthy and happy. Staying safe from crime, terrorism, and natural disasters. How can you *not* be anxious? Jesus said, "In this world you will have trouble" (John 16:33). In our lives, this can be an understatement!

It may not be easy to cope with anxiety. But not coping with your anxiety can make your life even harder. Anxiety can affect sleep, trigger physical illnesses, and interfere with daily functioning. What can you do to combat anxiety?

Jesus invites you to cast your anxieties upon Him. To trust in Him to take your burdens upon Himself. Pray to Jesus when you're feeling anxious and troubled. You'll experience an amazing peace that transcends all understanding. Find your peace in Jesus. He's the Prince of Peace.

Lord Jesus, we thank You for taking our burdens upon Yourself. Help us to cast our worries upon You so that Your peace will melt all our anxieties away. In Your precious name, amen.

Do not be anxious about anything, but in every situation, by prayer and petition, with thanksgiving, present your requests to God. And the peace of God, which transcends all understanding, will guard your hearts and your minds in Christ Jesus.

—PHILIPPIANS 4:6–7

FOR PRAYERFUL REFLECTION

How does Jesus help you cope with your anxieties and give you peace?

_____

_____

_____

34

JESUS IS MY PERFECT PARTNER

I will never let you down.

—JESUS

*N*O MATTER HOW good our relationships with loved ones, we can sometimes feel let down. No one can fulfill our needs all the time—except one Person.

Jesus knows you in ways others can't. He knit you in the womb. He knows the intimate recesses of your heart and even the number of hairs on your head. Jesus loves you in a way others don't—unconditionally. He understands when you mess up and keeps loving you anyway. Jesus forgives you in a way others don't. He died on the cross so that you could be forgiven. Jesus gives you the grace others have a hard time giving—grace that is unearned and undeserved. Jesus is present in ways others can't be. People come and go, but Jesus is in your life to stay. He was with you before you were born. He's with you every moment of every day. And He'll be with you for all eternity.

If you're looking for a person who will never let you down, turn to Jesus. He'll give you what others can't, don't, won't, and never will.

Lord Jesus, we thank You that You are our perfect partner. Help us to turn to You, knowing that You love us too much to ever let us down. In Your precious name, amen.

Be strong and courageous. Do not be afraid or terrified because of them, for the LORD your God goes with you; he will never leave you nor forsake you.
—DEUTERONOMY 31:6

FOR PRAYERFUL REFLECTION

In what ways is the Lord your perfect partner?

_____

_____

_____

35

JESUS IS MY "I CAN"

You can't, but I can.

—JESUS

*I*WAS IN THE supermarket the other day with my service dog, Zack. He was trotting happily beside my wheelchair wheels, as I headed for the tuna aisle. When I arrived at the Bumble Bee tuna, I couldn't reach the can. It was on too high a shelf. I stretched up to grab it but fell back into my seat in pain. I tried again and failed. Zack was getting antsy. I could tell he was impatient to get to the meat aisle to revel in the smell of fresh sausages.

Finally I saw someone in a branded blue coat. It was as if she were sent by God to help. I called out to her and asked for assistance. I was relieved when she handed me the can of tuna—but my ego was bruised. That's when the Lord reminded me of an important biblical truth. None of us can do it alone. Whether we're trying to reach a can of tuna or get through a major crisis. Whether we're completing a shopping list or fulfilling a bucket list. Whatever we hope to accomplish in life, we need His help along the way. Because when we can't—He can. He can even turn a can of tuna into a profound lesson on life. Now that's one amazing Lord!

Lord Jesus, we thank You that when we can't, You can. Enable us to humbly call out to You when we need help. And to be grateful for Your loving grace in our lives. In Your precious name, amen.

~ﾘﾙﾟ~

I am the vine; you are the branches. If you
remain in me and I in you, you will bear much
fruit; apart from me you can do nothing.
—John 15:5

For Prayerful Reflection

How does Jesus help you accomplish what you can't do on
your own?

_____

_____

_____

36

JESUS IS MY PERSEVERANCE

Stay the course in Me.

—JESUS

*I*T'S NOT EASY to persevere in life when you're going through trials. It can feel like your trudging endlessly through the muck and mire. Psychologists suggest several ways to increase your perseverance. Pursue something you really want. Set goals and devise a plan. Enlist the support of others. Believe in yourself. This is the secular meaning of perseverance—but it's not the biblical one.

According to the Bible, *perseverance* means to pursue a goal the Lord has chosen for you. To proceed according to His plan for your life. To pray to Him to support your efforts. To believe that He will help you do what you can't do alone. To press onward by the power of His grace. Perseverance in the Lord means staying the course even if you don't win laurels. Because in heaven you'll be rewarded with crowns!

Lord Jesus, we thank You that You help us through the trials and challenges of our lives. Enable us to press on and to persevere in You. In Your precious name, amen.

Blessed is the one who perseveres under trial because, having stood the test, that person will receive the crown of life that the Lord has promised to those who love him.

—JAMES 1:12

FOR PRAYERFUL REFLECTION

How do you persevere in the Lord?

_____

_____

_____

37

JESUS IS MY COMFORTER

I weep for you and with you.

—**JESUS**

ost of us have grieved the loss of a loved one. Dying is a natural part of life. Yet when the time inevitably comes, it's still very hard to face. We deny, get angry, become depressed, feel anxious and guilty, and attempt to bargain with God. The Bible tells us that there's "a time to weep and a time to laugh, a time to mourn and a time to dance" (Eccles. 3:4). Why does the Lord set aside a time for weeping and mourning? Because He knows that, while grief doesn't feel good, it's good for you.

Grieving enables you to heal. It not only gives your emotions a needed outlet, but it also allows you time to gain a valuable perspective on life. Grieving brings you closer to God, because He is close to the brokenhearted (Ps. 34:18).

Grief may feel like weakness, but it reflects great strength. So don't hold back. Allow yourself to grieve. Reach out to loved ones for support. Let the Lord take you in His care. Allow Him to strengthen you, comfort you, and help you readjust to life. Give yourself time to heal.

We all die. But in Jesus, we have new life in that far better place. Where there is no more death. No more grief. No more sorrow. Only joy—and joyful reunions!

Lord Jesus, we thank You that You died for us so that we can have eternal life. Help us to reach out to You in our grief so that we may be healed in You. In Your precious name, amen.

~ɔ☯ℓ~

Weeping may stay for the night, but
rejoicing comes in the morning.
—Psalm 30:5

For Prayerful Reflection

How does the Lord help you through your grief?

_____

_____

_____

38

JESUS IS MY VICTORY

In Me, you always win.

—JESUS

*W*HEN I WAKE up in the morning, I notice something troubling. Even though I can perform amazing gymnastics in my dreams, my real muscles don't work very well. They're painful, weak, and not ready for prime time. That's when I struggle most with acceptance.

It's not easy for any of us to accept pain, suffering, disappointments, and loss. Yet they're all part of life. I have to admit that I'm not a joyful sufferer. But I am a joyful believer. Believing that Jesus gives my life meaning despite my suffering. Believing that Jesus lifts me up despite my circumstances. Believing that when I am weak, I am strong in Him. Believing that there's a purpose to my life, despite all outward appearances. Believing that I can make every day a good day if I spend my day in Jesus.

It's difficult to accept trials in life. You can feel hopeless, helpless, and depressed. But you needn't despair. When you accept Jesus into your heart, you can become a joyful believer. No longer a victim, but a victor!

Lord Jesus, we thank You that, despite our circumstances, we can be victorious in You. Help us to rise in You every morning as joyful believers, knowing that You can make each day our best day. In Your precious name, amen.

I can do all this through him who gives me strength.
—PHILIPPIANS 4:13

FOR PRAYERFUL REFLECTION

How does being a joyful believer transform your days?

_____

_____

_____

39

JESUS IS MY ALL-WEATHER FRIEND

I am with you in good times and bad.

—JESUS

*I*T'S EASY TO believe in God on sunny days when the weather is fair, the sky is blue, and the winds are light. When you're healthy, happy, and content with your life. But when heavy weather blows in and you lose your health, your job, your money, or a cherished loved one, it's not as easy to hang onto faith. You may begin to question God's love, loyalty, and caring. You may even wonder whether He's really there at all.

Corrie ten Boom and her sister Betsie had every reason to feel abandoned by the Lord. Trapped in the midst of unimaginable suffering in a concentration camp during World War II, they could have easily lost their faith in Jesus and His love for them. Yet Betsie told Corrie just before she died: "There is no pit so deep that God's love is not deeper still."[1]

Jesus is not just with you on sunny days. He's also with you when your life is in the pits. When darkness overtakes you and all you feel is pain, grief, depression, and loss. You may lose sight of Him when clouds descend. But you can rest assured that Jesus never loses sight of you. He weathers the fierce winds and the pounding rains with you. Jesus is not your fair-weather friend. He's your all-weather friend.

Lord Jesus, we thank You that You're with us in good times and bad. Help us to cling onto You through the storms of our lives. Carry us through the wind and rain to the dawn of a new day. In Your precious name, amen.

ℑℚℓ

In the day when I cried out, You answered me, And
made me bold with strength in my soul.
—Psalm 138:3

For Prayerful Reflection

Think about a time when you went through a crisis. How were
you able to hold onto Jesus?

_____

_____

_____

40

JESUS IS MY TECHNICOLOR

I will fill you with wonder.

—JESUS

o you feel like you're spending time but missing the moment? You go to work, take care of the children, shop for food, pay the bills, go to sleep, and do it all over again the next day. Life can be a blur. Devoid of color, depth, and meaning.

Spend your moments in Jesus. You'll see the beauty in life, not just your burdens. You'll feel the wonder, not just the weight of your worries. You'll be in the "here and now," not concerned about before or after. You'll be in the "what is," not mired in the "what ifs." You'll have peace and contentment in the midst of struggles. You'll see your life in a whole new light, even in the midst of darkness. Spend your moments in Jesus—and your black-and-white existence will turn to Technicolor!

Lord Jesus, we thank You that You bring color, depth, and meaning to our everyday lives. Help us to enliven our lives by living our moments in You. In Your precious name, amen.

For the LORD Most High is awesome, the
great King over all the earth.
—PSALM 47:2

For Prayerful Reflection

How does Jesus bring living color into your life?

_____

_____

_____

41

JESUS IS MY LONGEVITY

In Me, you are ageless.

—JESUS

OW OLD ARE you? If you'd rather not say, I understand. Although I have no problem telling you how old I am. I'm eternal! If you're a believer in Jesus Christ, so are you. You don't have to wait until you get to heaven to become eternal. You're eternal now—ageless in the sight of God. Being eternal this side of heaven means being in the world but not of it. Loving God more than the things of this world. Valuing what lasts more than what doesn't. Working for crowns, not laurels. Storing up treasures in heaven, not on Earth. Giving to others, not just taking. Choosing righteousness over sin. It means glorifying God, not yourself. Listening to God's voice over your own. Trusting the Lord more than yourself. Being eternal means being blessed in ways too numerous to count. No matter how old you are, aren't you glad you're eternal?

Lord Jesus, we thank You that You made the ultimate sacrifice so that can we have eternal life. Help us to fix our eyes not on the things of Earth, but on the things of Heaven. Enable us to focus not on ourselves, but on You—our Savior! In Your precious name, amen.

For God so loved the world that he gave his one and only Son, that whoever believes in him shall not perish but have eternal life.
—JOHN 3:16

For Prayerful Reflection

How does being eternal affect how you live your life on Earth?

_____

_____

_____

42

JESUS IS MY WINGS

I will lift you up on eagles' wings.

—**JESUS**

*T*HE BIBLE IS filled with people—from Moses to Jesus—
who fell into despair while facing overwhelming challenges. And nothing has changed since then. Look around you. There are desperate people everywhere. Waiting for circumstances to change, while falling deeper into despair. Waiting for people to rescue them, while feeling increasingly abandoned and hopeless. Waiting for answers, while growing more and more weary.

When you're down and out, don't wait upon the things of this Earth to lift you up. Wait upon the Lord. Hope in Him. You will be strengthened. You will run and not get winded. You will walk and not be tired. He will lift you up on eagles' wings and carry you to new heights!

Lord Jesus, we thank You that You lift us up when we're down. Help us to find our hope in You. Give us the patience to wait upon You to lift us up on eagles' wings. In Your precious name, amen.

But those who hope in the LORD will renew their strength.
They will soar on wings like eagles; they will run and
not grow weary, they will walk and not be faint.
—ISAIAH 40:31

FOR PRAYERFUL REFLECTION

How does the Lord lift you up when you're down?

_____

_____

_____

43

JESUS IS MY SELF-WORTH

I know how much you're really worth.

—JESUS

*D*O YOU LACK self-worth? Maybe you wish you were smarter, richer, or better looking. Life on Earth can seem like a popularity contest that can leave you feeling like a loser in the eyes of others. But in God's eyes, you're a winner. You're His precious creation and His beloved child. He knitted you in the womb and made you for relationship with Him. He gave you unique talents and gifts and a special place in His kingdom.

The Lord doesn't judge you based upon money, IQ, or appearance. He judges you by the fruit of the Spirit: "love, joy, peace, forbearance, kindness, goodness, faithfulness, gentleness and self-control" (Gal. 5:22–23). The Lord looks at your heart to measure your true worth.

Value yourself as the Lord values you—by your good fruits, not by your good fortune—and watch how your self-worth skyrockets.

Lord Jesus, we thank You that while others may look at the outward appearance, You look at the heart. Help us to see our worth through Your eyes and to value ourselves as You value us. In Your precious name, amen.

The LORD does not look at the things people look at. People look at the outward appearance, but the LORD looks at the heart.
—1 SAMUEL 16:7

For Prayerful Reflection

What is the difference between how you value yourself and how God values you?

_____

_____

_____

44

JESUS IS MY "ALL IN"

I call you to be My instrument on Earth.

—JESUS

WHEN YOU FEEL the Lord prompting you to do something, are you all in? Are you ready to put your heart and soul into it? It's not always easy to rise to the occasion. To take the call, even when you know it's God calling. You may be burdened with responsibilities and commitments. You may feel tired, weak, and burned out.

Jim Elliot, a missionary who was murdered in Ecuador, wrote in his diary, "Wherever you are, be all there! Live to the hilt every situation you believe to be the will of God."[1] You may not be called to give the ultimate sacrifice. But whatever it is that God requires of you, be all in. You'll be surprised how much you get out of it. You'll experience meaning, purpose, and joy as never before. You'll do greater things than you ever thought possible. You'll experience the pleasure of the Lord in ways you could never have imagined.

Take God's call. Become His instrument on Earth. Use the gifts of grace that He has given you to bless the lives of others. You will be the one most blessed.

Lord, we thank You that we are Your instruments on Earth. Help us to joyfully accept Your call so that we may bless many lives for Your glory. In Your precious name, amen.

᠊ᢈᎦᏋ᠊

Each of you should use whatever gift you have
received to serve others, as faithful stewards
of God's grace in its various forms.
—1 PETER 4:10

For Prayerful Reflection

How does answering Jesus's call to bless others also bless you?

_____

_____

_____

45

JESUS IS MY BEST FRIEND FOREVER

I am your friend.

—JESUS

*T*HE WORLD HAS billions of people, but it's sometimes hard to find a really good friend. Someone who supports you and is always by your side. Who knows you better than you know yourself. Who loves you as you are and helps you to be the best you can be. Who is loyal and faithful. Who lifts you up and won't let you down. Who always puts you first. Who listens to you, prays for you, stands up for you, and would die for you. If you're searching for such a friend, you needn't worry. He's already found you.

Jesus—the all-knowing, all-powerful, and all-loving Lord and Creator—is your friend. How awesome is that! You can reciprocate by being the kind of friend to Him that He is to you. Be loyal, faithful, and attentive. Put Him first in your life, just as He puts you first in His. Be the best friend you can possibly be to Him. And you'll have the best friendship you can possibly have in this world and the next. Because Jesus is your best friend forever.

Lord Jesus, we thank You for being our friend. Help us to honor Your friendship by always putting You first in our lives. In Your precious name, amen.

I have called you friends.
—JOHN 15:15

For Prayerful Reflection

In what ways is Jesus your best friend forever?

_____

_____

_____

46

JESUS IS MY MASTER TEACHER

I teach you life lessons.

—JESUS

*T*HE LORD NOT only made summer, fall, winter, and spring. He also made the seasons of your life. Not just from infancy to old age but also the less predictable seasons. The seasons that happen when you least expect them. Your spouse dies too young. Your health fails at age thirty. You lose your job at the height of your success, in the prime of your life. It's like a blizzard blasting through your life on a warm summer day. And you're left with two nagging questions: Why did this happen to me? And why now?

You may not be able to understand God's timing or His reasons. But each season has its lessons to teach—and it's your job to master their wisdom. When you do, you'll become wise beyond your years. You'll see the blessings, not your brokenness. The opportunities, not your obstacles. The gains, not your losses. The triumphs, not your tragedies. You'll rest easy in God's promises of a new season of hope and healing!

Lord Jesus, we thank You for teaching us life lessons. Help us to be faithful learners. Enable us to grow in wisdom and to mature beyond our years. In Your precious name, amen.

~இல்~

To every thing there is a season, and a time
to every purpose under the heaven.
—ECCLESIASTES 3:1, KJV

FOR PRAYERFUL REFLECTION

Have you experienced unexpected seasons in your life? How have you grown from them?

_____

_____

_____

47

JESUS IS MY RESPITE

Take a break with Me.

—JESUS

*I*N OUR HECTIC and complicated lives, we scramble to meet pressing demands, deadlines, and commitments every day. How can we possibly find time to take a break with the Lord for needed respite?

When Jesus walked the earth, He had even greater responsibilities. Traveling from town to town to preach. Tending to the needs of thousands. Performing healings and miracles. Yet, when He felt exhausted and spent, He still found time to take a break. He retreated to a remote area to rest, reflect, and pray. In the stillness, He found blessed communion with the Father.

When you're feeling tired and overwhelmed, take a break with Jesus. Your mission will seem clearer and your priorities straighter. Your mind will be calmer and your heart more peaceful. Your soul will be refreshed and you'll be ready to reengage. You'll return to the world with a clearer purpose, knowing why you're doing what you're doing. You'll make better decisions based upon God's will, not your own.

Jesus, who accomplished the most important work in history, took time out to take a break with His Father. So give yourself a break—and take a break with Jesus.

Lord Jesus, we thank You that You are our respite in our hectic and complicated lives. Help us to take a break with You for rest, reflection, prayer, and blessed communion. In Your precious name, amen.

Jesus often withdrew to lonely places and prayed.
—LUKE 5:16

For Prayerful Reflection

How are your breaks with Jesus crucial in your life?

_____

_____

_____

48

JESUS IS MY DELIVERER

I have great plans for you.

—JESUS

O YOU SOMETIMES feel like you have nowhere to turn and nothing to do but to give up? You're not alone. Even Jesus had His share of hard times when He came to Earth. People turned against Him, persecuted Him, mocked Him, and tortured Him. Just before He was crucified, Jesus was so distraught that "his sweat was like drops of blood falling to the ground" (Luke 22:44). But Jesus didn't give up. Instead He did something so miraculous that it resonates to this very day. He gave in. Fulfilling God's plan by willingly going to the cross to save us from our sins. Can you imagine how different our lives would be if Jesus hadn't given in?

When you're on the verge of quitting, don't give up. Give in—and give it up to the Lord. To His wisdom, His will, and His perfect plan for your life. When you have nowhere to turn, let the Lord turn things around for you. There's nothing wrong with giving in—when you give it up to the Lord.

Lord Jesus, we thank You that You chose to suffer and die for us. When we're on the verge of giving up, enable us to give in and give it up to You. Help us to proclaim, "Your will be done!" In Your precious name, amen.

⸙

"For I know the plans I have for you," declares
the LORD, "plans to prosper you and not to harm
you, plans to give you hope and a future."
—JEREMIAH 29:11

FOR PRAYERFUL REFLECTION

Recall a time when you gave in and gave it up to the Lord. What was the result?

_____

_____

_____

49

JESUS IS MY REMEDY

I can fix your broken life.

—JESUS

*H*AS YOUR LIFE ever become so broken that you doubted even God could fix it? Maybe you lost a loved one and wondered how your hurting heart could ever heal. Or a cherished relationship went sour and you couldn't imagine how you could ever love again. Or you declared bankruptcy and you couldn't envision how you could ever financially recover. Or you were diagnosed with an incurable disease and you didn't think you could ever regain your health.

I have to confess that sometimes I wonder if I will be cured of this neuromuscular disease. Then I look to the west and see the majesty of the Rockies. I look up and see the splendor of star-filled skies. I look beyond and imagine the billions of galaxies in the universe—all created by God's hand!

You may feel that your problems aren't fixable. That you are limited by your circumstances. But look around. There's no limit to what God can do. He can redeem your losses and turn them into gains. He can introduce new opportunities that will turn your life around. He can bring about a brand-new beginning, just when you think you're at the end. Praise God that when we can't do anything to fix our circumstances, He can do everything!

Lord Jesus, we thank You for mending our broken lives with Your infinite power. We're so grateful that You, who made the universe, take time to make our lives whole. Help us to replace our hopelessness with hopeful expectation, knowing that You are our blessed remedy. In Your precious name, amen.

∽ℐℰ∾

Great is our Lord and mighty in power;
his understanding has no limit.
—PSALM 147:5

FOR PRAYERFUL REFLECTION

How has the Lord fixed what's broken in your life?

_____

_____

_____

50

JESUS IS MY ANSWER TO SUFFERING

I am your hope, your comfort, and your strength.

—JESUS

WHY DO BAD things happen to good people? Disease, bankruptcy, broken marriages, and the death of loved ones. There's plenty of suffering to go around. Even Jesus suffered when He came to Earth.

Some people think that good people suffer because God is not powerful enough. Then how could He have created the universe? Others think that He's not loving enough. Then why did He suffer and die for us? Still others believe that God isn't involved in our lives. Then how could He possibly know everything about us—even the number of hairs on our head?

I have no doubt that God is powerful, loving, and involved in our lives. But why does He allow good people to suffer? The answer is not a "why" but a "who." Someone who came to earth to walk among us. To share in our suffering. To weep for us. And to suffer and die for us in the ultimate act of sacrificial love. The answer to suffering is Jesus Christ.

Jesus is the strength in our suffering. The hope in our despair. The blessing in our brokenness. We may never know why bad things happen to good people. But we know the "who." And that makes all the difference!

Lord Jesus, we thank You that, in times of suffering, You are always with us, comforting us, strengthening us, and weeping with us. We don't know why we suffer. But we do know that You are the answer to our suffering. And, for that, we are humbly and eternally grateful. In Your precious name, amen.

~oße~

He heals the brokenhearted and binds up their wounds.
—Psalm 147:3

For Prayerful Reflection

In what ways has Jesus been the blessing in your brokenness?

_____

_____

_____

51

JESUS IS MY RESCUER

You can depend on Me.

—JESUS

*D*ID YOU EVER wonder why God sometimes waits until the last minute before He rescues you? Things keep getting worse. You feel more and more helpless. More and more hopeless. Just when all seems lost, God shows up. Like the sheriff in an Old West movie, who frees a poor fellow tied to the railroad tracks just before he's run over by a speeding train.

Waiting for God can feel like a nail-biter. Why does the Lord sometimes wait so long before He acts? Maybe it's because He wants us to admit that, just as we needed Jesus to save us from our sins, we need His grace in our daily lives. We need His help, His guidance, and His rescue. We just can't do it alone.

When you're waiting for the Lord, remember His promises. Things may look grim and hopeless, but God will come through. He always does and always will.

Lord Jesus, we thank You for rescuing us in times of trouble. Help us to be patient and to acknowledge our dependence on You to bring about the perfect solutions in our lives. In Your precious name, amen.

Then they cried out to the LORD in their trouble,
and he delivered them from their distress.
—PSALM 107:6

FOR PRAYERFUL REFLECTION

In what ways does the Lord rescue you?

_____

_____

_____

52

JESUS IS MY SECOND CHANCE

In My eyes, you're not a failure.

—**JESUS**

*W*E ALL FAIL at one time or another. We're fallen human beings who make mistakes. We disappoint ourselves, other people, and God. But even though we fail, it doesn't mean we're failures.

People thought Jesus was a failure when they saw Him die on the cross. When He whispered the words, "It is finished," everyone thought He was. No one could have imagined that it wasn't the end but the beginning. That it wasn't a defeat but a victory. Jesus overcame death so that you could have eternal life. He overcame darkness so that you could be cleansed of your sins. He succeeded so that you would never be a failure.

You can claim the victory Jesus won for you. Put Jesus first in your life, and you'll have a second chance when you fail. A chance to confess and repent. To be rescued by the Lord's mercy, grace, and forgiveness. To learn and grow from your mistakes. To turn your failures into successes. To use your God-given talents and abilities for the good. You may fail— but you'll never be a failure. Because in Jesus, you're already a success.

Lord Jesus, we thank You for the victory You won for us. Help us put You first in our lives so that when we fail, we will always have a second chance. In Your precious name, amen.

But thanks be to God! He gives us the victory through our Lord Jesus Christ.
—1 CORINTHIANS 15:57

FOR PRAYERFUL REFLECTION

What second chances has Jesus give you?

_____

_____

_____

53

JESUS IS MY CUSHION

Fall into Me.

—JESUS

HEN YOU BEGIN a new day, you may worry what you will encounter along the way. If you're like me, you wish you could prepare yourself for whatever will befall you. My mother had a favorite expression: "If I knew where I'd fall, I'd put a pillow." If only we could line our path with pillows!

You may not be able to put a pillow where you fall. But Jesus gives you something even better. Someone who cushions the blows, absorbs the hurts, and enables you to rise again. He gives you nothing less than Himself.

Jesus is your cushion. Fall back on Him. He'll give you comfort, reassurance, and the strength to carry on. He'll even carry you when you lose your footing—until you can get back on your feet. C. S. Lewis wrote, "Relying on God has to begin all over again every day as if nothing had yet been done."[1] No matter what happens along the way today, isn't it comforting to know that you have the Lord of the universe to fall back on?

Lord Jesus, we thank You that You cushion our blows. Help us to rely on You when we fall. Lift us up, brush us off, and help us start all over again. In Your precious name, amen.

For I am the LORD your God who takes hold of your right hand and says to you, Do not fear; I will help you.
—ISAIAH 41:13

FOR PRAYERFUL REFLECTION

How does Jesus cushion the blows in your life?

_____

_____

_____

54

JESUS IS MY UNCONDITIONAL LOVE

I love you—no matter what.

—JESUS

*I*F YOU'RE LIKE me, there are times when it's hard to love yourself. When all you see are your flaws, flub ups, and failures. You may even wonder how anyone else can possibly love you.

Jesus loves you. Not because you're lovable, easy to love, or deserve to be loved. Jesus loves you not because of who you are—but because of who He is. He loves you because He *is* love. What better way is there for Him to express the enormity of His love than to love a sinner? Someone who is hard to love. Who isn't perfect and 100 percent lovable.

When you feel unlovable, don't despair. Jesus will always love you—even at those times when you're unlovable. Now that's amazing love!

Lord Jesus, we thank You for Your amazing love. Help us to strive to be more worthy of Your love. Enable us to become more like You, so that we may honor Your love every day. In Your precious name, amen.

This is love: not that we loved God, but that he loved us and sent his Son as an atoning sacrifice for our sins.
—1 JOHN 4:10

FOR PRAYERFUL REFLECTION

What does it mean to you to know that Jesus loves you even when you're unlovable?

_____

_____

_____

55

JESUS IS MY EQUIPPER

In Me, you can do more than you ever thought possible.

—JESUS

*I*T CAN BE hard to stay confident when you're going through life's challenges. You look around and see others who seem stronger, smarter, more articulate, and more talented. Yet the Bible is filled with people who seemed the least qualified to accomplish the great things they did. Moses, a stutterer, challenged powerful Pharaoh and won, freeing his people from Egyptian oppression. David, a shepherd boy, faced off against the giant Goliath and was victorious.

When I wrote my first book, I was an unknown author lying in bed with a progressive disease. The odds of getting a book published were less than 2 percent. I knew no one in the publishing industry. I had no platform. Everyone doubted I could become a published author, and sadly, so did I. Yet God knew what no one else knew. He had set me on a mission that would come to fruition by His grace.

God is calling you to be more than you think you can be and to do more than you think you can do. Whether you're persevering through your own trials or helping others through theirs, God has equipped you for the task. So face your challenges head on and keep on going. You may not believe you can do it. You may feel inadequate or weak. But call upon the power of the Lord— and you'll see what extraordinary things you can do in Him!

Lord Jesus, we thank You that You equip us for whatever we face in life. Help us to draw upon Your power, strength, and confidence in us. So that we can do more than we ever thought possible. In Your precious name, amen.

~ｏｏｅ~

Now may the God of peace…equip you with
everything good for doing his will, and may he
work in us what is pleasing to him, through Jesus
Christ, to whom be glory for ever and ever. Amen.
—HEBREWS 13:20–21

FOR PRAYERFUL REFLECTION

How does the Lord equip you to accomplish great things in
your life?

_____

_____

_____

56

JESUS IS MY REAL HOME

You always fit in with Me.

—JESUS

*I*F YOU FEEL like you don't fit in, don't despair. This world can be an alienating place. Jesus knew that all too well. When Jesus came to Earth, He didn't fit in. He was mocked, scorned, rejected, and ultimately killed. Yet those who also didn't fit in—the sick, the outcasts, and the tax collectors—fit in perfectly with Jesus.

Jesus makes a special place for you with Him where you always fit in. Where you're loved, supported, valued, and appreciated for who you are. A place where you're never alone. Where you can find meaning and higher purpose for your life. Where you can use your gifts and talents to the max for the best.

Take your place with Jesus. Walk with Him every day. You'll never feel like an outsider again.

Lord Jesus, we thank You that You make a special place for us with You. Help us to fit you into all the moments of our lives, just as You fit us into Yours. Because in You we always fit! In Your precious name, amen.

And Jesus replied, "Foxes have dens and birds have nests, but the Son of Man has no place to lay his head."
—LUKE 9:58

For Prayerful Reflection

In what ways do you fit in with Jesus more than with anyone else?

_____

_____

_____

57

JESUS IS MY RISING UP

I will lift you above your circumstances.

—JESUS

HERE WAS A time when my neuromuscular disease was getting the best of me, and I just couldn't hang on any longer. I lost my grip and had to let go. I expected to hit bottom and crash hard. That's when I called out to Jesus—and something strange happened.

I started to rise. Up and up I went until I was high above my circumstances. I looked down at my huge problems, and they suddenly seemed so small. I saw tidal waves of trials become mere ripples and mountains of misery turn into molehills. Held in Jesus's grasp, I felt myself transformed. From weak to strong. From powerless to powerful. I knew that I could overcome whatever challenges I faced—all by His loving grace.

When you're in free fall, call upon the Lord. He will lift you up. He will help you overcome your overwhelming problems. He will give you strength in your weakness and empower you in ways nothing else can or ever will this side of heaven.

Lord Jesus, we thank You that You're with us in times of struggle. Help us to call out to You when we're falling, so that You can powerfully lift us up. In Your precious name, amen.

But he said to me, "My grace is sufficient for you, for my power is made perfect in weakness." Therefore I will boast all the more gladly about my weaknesses, so that Christ's power may rest on me.
—2 CORINTHIANS 12:9

FOR PRAYERFUL REFLECTION

In what ways does Jesus empower you to overcome the trials in your life?

_____

_____

_____

58

JESUS IS MY JOY

Rejoice in the Holy Spirit!

—JESUS

*I*N A LIFE filled with challenges and trials, it's easy to feel despondent. Yet the Bible tells us that we should be joyful. How can we be joyful when we're down in the dumps?

Jesus knew how hard life can be. He experienced trials firsthand when He walked the Earth. So, when He departed, He left us with a powerful remedy that filled Him with abundant joy—and will do the same for you.

The Holy Spirit is a wondrous source of true joy in this world, given to you by the grace of Jesus Christ. Why is this gift so special? Because joy is not the same as happiness. Joy is a fruit of the Holy Spirit, resulting from God's work in you. Joy isn't fleeting. It doesn't come from things outside yourself. Joy comes from the very presence of God deep inside you. Joy strengthens you in trials and helps you to overcome. Joy can even increase your well-being. The Bible tells us, "A cheerful heart is good medicine, but a crushed spirit dries up the bones" (Prov. 17:22). Joy can enhance your life in so many ways. But the height of joy is being in relationship with Jesus Christ—your everlasting source of joy!

Lord Jesus, we thank You for Your gift of the Holy Spirit. Help us to be lifted up by the joy You have planted in our hearts. May we rejoice in the Spirit always! In Your precious name, amen.

Rejoice in the Lord always. I will say it again: Rejoice!
—PHILIPPIANS 4:4

FOR PRAYERFUL REFLECTION

How do you experience the joy of the Holy Spirit in you?

_____

_____

_____

59

JESUS IS MY MAKEOVER

I will make you new.

—JESUS

ID YOU EVER wish you could get a really good make-over? The kind that would cause your friends to say, "Gee, I hardly recognize you!" You can—and you don't even have to go to the spa.

When you accept Jesus into your heart, you are made new. Transformed from the inside out, as you continue to grow in His likeness. You become beautiful, not only in His sight but also in the sight of others.

After I accepted Christ, so many people told me I looked so much better—healthy, vibrant, and alive. I was still sitting in a wheelchair with a neuromuscular disease. But what they saw was not just me. They also saw the light of Jesus shining though me.

If you're looking for the ultimate makeover, don't go to the spa. Go to Jesus. He will make you brand-new. He'll give you a makeover so amazing that when you look in the mirror, you'll be a beautiful reflection of the Lord for all to see!

Lord Jesus, we thank You that You transform us from the inside out and make us vibrant and alive. Help us to be a beautiful reflection of You. In Your precious name, amen.

Therefore, if anyone is in Christ, the new creation
has come: The old has gone, the new is here!
—2 CORINTHIANS 5:17

For Prayerful Reflection

In what ways does the light of Jesus shine through you to others?

_____

_____

_____

60

JESUS IS MY MEANING

You're meant for relationship with Me.

—**JESUS**

*S*OMETIMES LIFE CAN seem meaningless. You get up in the morning, go to work, take care of the children, and pay your bills. Weeks turn into months, and months turn into years. When you look back, you may wonder where the time went—and what it all meant.

When you can't find meaning in life, don't despair. Your life already has meaning. You're a child of God, made for relationship with Him for His pleasure and purpose. What could be more meaningful than that?

If you're looking for meaning in life, find your meaning in Jesus. He'll give you the meaning you're missing. The pleasure you're lacking. The purpose you're craving. In Him, everything you do will matter—how you do your job, raise the children, and treat your friends. Because when you live according to God's will, all your actions ultimately honor Him.

Live in the will of the Lord, and you'll never have to question again what your life truly means. You'll already know!

Lord Jesus, we thank You that our lives mean something because we are Your children and mean so very much to You. Help us to honor our blessed relationship with You by doing Your will every day. In Your precious name, amen.

_ॐ_

Yet to all who did receive him, to those who believed
in his name, he gave the right to become children of
God—children born not of natural descent, nor of
human decision or a husband's will, but born of God.
—JOHN 1:12–13

FOR PRAYERFUL REFLECTION

In what ways does your relationship with Jesus bring meaning
to your life?

_____

_____

_____

61

JESUS IS MY FAMILY

You are My precious family.

—JESUS

*I*N OUR SOCIETY, it's easy to believe that you're on your own. Lost in the masses of humanity in an increasingly competitive world. But you needn't feel alone. You're part of a family. A member of an amazing body of believers known as the body of Christ. The Lord has endowed you with unique talents and gifts. You matter. You can make a difference.

Even though I live alone, I don't feel alone. I feel the full embrace of my family in the body of Christ. Lifting me up, praying for me, and encouraging me day by day. Supporting me in my ministry and inspiring me to continue writing for the Lord.

If you feel alone, don't despair. Claim your place in His loving family—the body of Christ. Give and be given to. Pray and be prayed for. Encourage and be encouraged. Inspire and be inspired. You will be blessed as you richly bless others.

When you join with other believers, the power of the body of Christ is limitless— unleashing a flood of loving power into the world unlike anything else on Earth.

Lord Jesus, we thank You that we are members of Your loving family of believers. Help us to join together to make a difference in each other's lives in this dark and fallen world. In Your precious name, amen.

Joe

Now you are the body of Christ, and
each one of you is a part of it.
—1 CORINTHIANS 12:27

For Prayerful Reflection

In what ways does being a member of the body of Christ make a difference in your life?

_____

_____

_____

JESUS IS MY FRIEND PROVIDER

I give you friends. Love them as you love yourself.
—JESUS

D O YOU KNOW why God gives you friends? You may think it's because He doesn't want you to be lonely. That may be true for secular friends. But Christian friends have a far greater purpose.

Christian friends walk alongside you on your faith journey. They give you encouragement, inspiration, and strength. They pray for you and grow with you. They keep you on the straight and narrow and gently lead you back to the path when you stray. They can be trusted with your deepest thoughts, fondest dreams, and greatest hopes. They're always there for you—in good times and bad. But there's something even more special about Christian friends. They're part of God's perfect plan for you. Coming into your life at just the right time and place to richly bless you.

Christian friends are treasures to be cherished. They're truly a gift from God!

Lord Jesus, we thank You that You give us Christian friends. Help us to treasure them as special gifts from You. Help us to be as good a friend to them as they are to us. In Your precious name, amen.

Greater love has no one than this: to lay
down one's life for one's friends.
—JOHN 15:13

For Prayerful Reflection

How do your Christian friends bless your life?

_____

_____

_____

63

JESUS IS MY LIVING WATER

I will quench your thirst.

—JESUS

*I*T'S NOT ALWAYS easy to sustain faith when you're wrestling with life's challenges. We all face periods when we feel terribly spent and discouraged.

When I was a new Christian, I was filled to the brim with joy. I could feel the Holy Spirit in my heart. I could feel the presence of Jesus in my soul. But sadly, the honeymoon was soon over. My spiritual satiation was replaced with thirst.

We all have dry times. Even Mother Teresa struggled with spiritual dryness. Yet she remained faithful. Why? Because she realized that, while God may seem to be silent, He's never absent.

Jesus knows how hard it is for you to trudge through the deserts of life. So He gives you an awesome remedy. One so miraculous that it can only come from the Holy Spirit. It's an oasis in the desert to quench your dry spirit. A potion to refresh your soul. An elixir to replenish your strength. It's called living water— and it's not just a temporary fix. It's a perpetual spring rising up inside you, giving you eternal life. So when you're tired and spiritually spent, have a drink of living water. You'll be amazed at how refreshed you'll be!

Lord Jesus, we thank You for Your gift of living water. A remarkable elixir that gives us strength, replenishes our soul, and imparts to us eternal life. Lead us to Your well of living water when we're weary and spiritually dry. So that we may be restored and renewed. In Your precious name, amen.

~oe~

Jesus answered her, "If you knew the gift of God and
who it is that asks you for a drink, you would have
asked him and he would have given you living water."
—JOHN 4:10

FOR PRAYERFUL REFLECTION

What do you do to replenish your faith when you're spiritually dry?

_____

_____

_____

64

JESUS IS MY IMPOSSIBLE MADE POSSIBLE

Nothing is impossible for Me.

—JESUS

*H*AVE YOU EVER had a dream so big that you never thought it would come true? You're in good company. Joseph was sold into slavery by his jealous brothers but rose to become the lord of Pharaoh's entire household. Sarah thought she was too old to give birth but bore a beautiful baby boy at age ninety. Jesus was mocked, tortured, and killed but rose to become the Savior of billions of people. Your dreams may seem impossible to you. But God can make the impossible possible. There's no such thing as an impossible dream when your dream is God's dream for you.

So dream big. Pray continuously with a sincere heart and pure intentions. Strive to discern God's will. Show up, work hard, and don't give up. Allow God to work through you, and you'll be blessed beyond your wildest dreams. In Jesus, you can never dream big enough!

Lord Jesus, we thank You that You make the impossible possible. Help us to maintain our hope in You and to never give up on our dreams. Enable us to make our dreams come true, in accordance with Your perfect will. In Your precious name, amen.

Jesus looked at them and said, "With man this is impossible, but with God all things are possible."
—MATTHEW 19:26

FOR PRAYERFUL REFLECTION

Recall a time in your life when the Lord made the impossible possible. How did the Lord make your dream a reality?

_____

_____

_____

65

JESUS IS MY MASTER PLANNER

I have the perfect plan for your life.

—JESUS

ID YOU EVER ask, "Why on Earth do I have to go through this?" When difficulties arise that are not in your plan, don't despair. They may turn out to be part of a far greater plan.

The last thing Noah wanted to do was to build a huge ark on a sunny day. Yet, through him, God saved humanity. The last thing Moses wanted to do was confront the powerful Pharaoh of Egypt. Yet, through Him, God saved His people. The last thing Jesus wanted to do was to die the most painful of deaths on a cross. He begged, "Father, if you are willing, take this cup from me" (Luke 22:42). Yet, through Him, God saved us from our sins and reconciled us to Him.

When you're going through trials, don't despair. God may be planning to use what seems to be the worst thing that can happen to you for the best. So walk in God's will. He works all things for the good of those who love Him.

Lord Jesus, we thank You that You turn our trials into triumphs. Help us to graciously accept what happens in our lives. And to say, "Not my will, but Your will be done!" In Your precious name, amen.

And we know that in all things God works
for the good of those who love him, who have
been called according to his purpose.
—ROMANS 8:28

For Prayerful Reflection

How has the Lord turned your trials into triumphs?

_____

_____

_____

66

JESUS IS MY GRACE

My grace I freely give to you.

—JESUS

*T*HERE'S ALWAYS SOMETHING to gripe about in life. Yet the Bible tells us to be thankful. It's not always easy to be thankful when you're facing trials. It's easier to gripe than to be grateful. But no matter how hard life is, there's also always something to be thankful for. Because, no matter how grumpy we get or how much we gripe, God is always gracious. Loving us in ways we may not feel at the moment. Providing for us in ways we may not immediately see.

Recently several of the wheels on my wheelchair broke at the same time. "What is this, a wheel epidemic?" I muttered. Because they were German made, the wheels had to be sent overseas for repair. I faced being stranded with no mobility for months. All I could do was gripe. But the Lord had a different plan in mind. Days after I sent the wheels, I received an unexpected call from the wheelchair mechanic. He just happened to encounter someone who could provide me with loaner wheels. It was no coincidence. God had met my griping with grace.

Max Lucado writes, "We indwell a garden of grace. God's love sprouts around us like lilacs and towers over us like Georgia pines, but we go on weed hunts. How many flowers do we miss in the process?"[1] When you're in the weeds and can't see one flower anywhere in sight, be grateful anyway. Not only for what you do have. But also for the abundance of seeds God is graciously planting at that very moment—just for you!

Lord Jesus, we thank You that, despite our griping, You are always gracious. Help us to gripe less and be grateful more. To embrace Your abundant grace. To trust that, even now, You are planting the seeds that will blossom into beautiful flowers to fill the gardens of our lives. In Your precious name, amen.

Let us then approach God's throne of grace with confidence, so that we may receive mercy and find grace to help us in our time of need.
—HEBREWS 4:16

FOR PRAYERFUL REFLECTION

In what ways has the Lord met your griping with grace?

_____

_____

_____

67

JESUS IS MY BEAUTY IN NATURE

I surround you with life-giving beauty.

—JESUS

*T*HE LORD'S CREATION is beautiful to behold. But did you know that it can also enhance your well-being? Explore the wonders of nature and you may find your energy increasing, your health improving, your mood lifting, your mental efficiency sharpening, and your stress decreasing. The silence of nature can be amazingly restorative. The sights of nature can be rejuvenating and uplifting. Best of all, nature is a great place to commune with the Lord. You'll see Him in the mountains, seas, sky, and sun. You'll be spiritually filled—and find blessed peace and solace in His awesome presence.

So get out! And while you're there, thank the Lord for His love and abundant grace in creating such a magnificent place!

Lord, we thank You for the beauty of Your creation and the well-being it brings. Help us to get off the couch and into the woods. To commune with You in the wonders of nature, which enliven our bodies and restore our souls. In Your precious name, amen.

The heavens declare the glory of God; the
skies proclaim the work of his hands.
—PSALM 19:1

For Prayerful Reflection

How does spending time in nature restore your soul?

_____

_____

_____

68

JESUS IS MY SOLID ROCK

Stand your ground in Me.

—JESUS

*I*T'S NOT EASY to keep your footing under the weight of the many burdens in life. It can feel like you're standing on sinking sand. In our society, people resort to a number of tactics to avoid sinking. They dig in their heels and keep doing what they're doing while hoping for the best. They rally the support of others. Some go into therapy. But there's another way to avoid sinking. One that is tried and true—and will never fail you.

Stand on the solid rock of Jesus Christ. Jesus can give you what nothing else in this world can. Sure footing in a world of sinking sand. Fortitude to stand your ground. Courage to combat temptation. Wisdom to choose the best course of action. Strength to carry on. Stand on the solid rock of Jesus— and you will never sink.

Lord Jesus, we thank You that You are our solid rock. Help us to find sure footing in You. In Your precious name, amen.

If you do not stand firm in your
faith, you will not stand at all.
—ISAIAH 7:9

FOR PRAYERFUL REFLECTION

Recall a time when you were on sinking sand. How did you find sure footing on the solid rock of Jesus Christ?

_____

_____

_____

69

JESUS IS MY DESTINATION

I am your safe harbor.

—JESUS

WHEN YOU'RE GOING through difficult times, where can you find Jesus? Pastor Charles Stanley writes, "As you walk through the valley of the unknown, you will find the footprints of Jesus both in front of you and beside you."[1] How comforting it is to know that Jesus not only leads us, but He also walks alongside us. Yet Jesus does even more.

Jesus makes Himself your destination. A safe harbor in the storm. Where you can unburden yourself and find comfort, healing, and blessed peace. A sanctuary unlike any other place this side of heaven.

When you're hurting, find your healing in Jesus. Call out to Him. He'll lead you on the right path—all the way to Himself. He'll wrap His arms around you in a loving embrace. He'll ease your pain with His presence. Make your destination Jesus. You'll find that there's no better place to be!

Lord Jesus, we thank You that You never forsake us. Help us to call out to You when we're hurting. Lead us to You so that we can find blessed peace and healing. In Your precious name, amen.

The LORD himself goes before you and will be with you; he will never leave you nor forsake you. Do not be afraid; do not be discouraged.

—DEUTERONOMY 31:8

For Prayerful Reflection

How do you make Jesus your destination?

_____

_____

_____

70

JESUS IS MY EYE IN THE STORM

I am your refuge.

—JESUS

A SUDDEN CRISIS CAN feel like a hurricane blasting through your life. You're pounded by fierce winds. Soaked by driving rains. You see your life being blown apart. Where can you take refuge?

When I first became ill, I lost everything. My life was in shambles. I didn't know how to pick up the pieces and go on—until I met Jesus Christ. He not only helped me put the pieces together. He also gave me blessed peace.

There's a place in a hurricane where the weather is clear, the winds are light, the sky is blue, and the sun is shining. Jesus waits for you there in the eye of the storm. In that blessed place, He holds you firmly in His grasp. He protects you from the battering winds and shelters you from the torrential rains. Suddenly all is calm. And in His amazing peace, you know that things will work out for the best. Because Jesus works all things for the good of those who love Him.

When you're facing storms in your life, battle through the wind and rain to reach Jesus. Where else can you find blessed peace in the midst of a raging storm?

Lord Jesus, we thank You that You're with us through the storms of our lives. Help us to find refuge in You. To get out of the weather and into the peaceful eye of the storm—where You wait for us. In Your precious name, amen.

_)0l,

God is our refuge and strength, an ever-present
help in trouble. Therefore we will not fear, though
the earth give way and the mountains fall into the
heart of the sea, though its waters roar and foam
and the mountains quake with their surging.
—Psalm 46:1–3

For Prayerful Reflection

Recall a stormy time in your life. How were you able to find
refuge and peace in Jesus?

_____

_____

_____

71

JESUS IS MY GOOD SHEPHERD

I will find you when you wander.

—JESUS

*I*T'S NOT EASY to remain steadfast in Jesus. Obstacles can so easily obscure your view that you may lose sight of Him just when you need Him most. Peter, Jesus's faithful disciple, disowned his Lord and Savior three times on the night of Jesus's arrest. If that could happen to Peter, what hope is there for the rest of us?

Our hope lies in Jesus Christ. Our Lord, the Good Shepherd, knows how easy it is for His sheep to stray. So He faithfully goes after the one in a hundred that has wandered away. When He brings it back to the fold, He rejoices over it more than the ninety-nine others.

You may lose sight of Jesus at times. But Jesus, who came to save the lost, will never lose sight of you. You may go astray. But Jesus will not rest until He brings you back into the fold. You're never lost when you have the Good Shepherd in your life. In Him, you're found!

Lord Jesus, we thank You that, even when we take our eyes off You, You never lose sight of us. Help us to keep our eyes firmly fixed on You. And when we lose sight of You, enable us to trust that You will lead us back into the fold. In Your precious name, amen.

What do you think? If a man owns a hundred sheep, and one of them wanders away, will he not leave the ninety-nine on the hills and go to look for the one that wandered off?
—MATTHEW 18:12

For Prayerful Reflection

Recall a time when you lost sight of Jesus. How did you return to the fold?

_____

_____

_____

72

JESUS IS MY WILLING EAR

Come to Me with a faithful heart, and I will listen.

—JESUS

*W*HEN I PRACTICED as a licensed clinical psychologist, I heard one complaint more than any other: "I don't feel heard." A wife didn't feel that her husband heard her feelings. A husband didn't feel that his wife heard his needs. Children didn't feel that their parents heard their dreams. Employees didn't feel that their bosses heard their problems. Sometimes it seemed that the only reason clients came to me was to find someone who would listen.

It can be hard to find someone to listen to you in this hectic world. Yet the Lord's love is so great that He will gladly take time out to listen. He longs to hear from you because He made you, loves you, delights in you, and desires relationship with you.

The next time you're looking around for someone to listen, look up. The Lord is waiting for you to tell Him your joys, sorrows, dreams, and dilemmas. Go to Him with an obedient, righteous, humble, and faithful heart. You can rest assured that He will not only faithfully listen—but also truly hear you.

Lord Jesus, we thank You that You always lend a willing ear. Help us to call upon You when we're looking for someone to listen. So that we can truly be heard. In Your precious name, amen.

We know that God does not listen to sinners. He listens to the godly person who does his will.
—JOHN 9:31

For Prayerful Reflection

In what ways do you feel heard by the Lord?

_____

_____

_____

73

JESUS IS MY LIGHTHOUSE

I will light your path to Me.

—JESUS

HEN I'M IN pain, exhausted, and weak from the symptoms of this neuromuscular disease, I can sometimes lose sight of the Lord. My suffering blinds me from seeing His light. That's when I search for a blessed beacon breaking through the darkness, pointing me back to Him. In that extraordinary light, I can see Him watching over me, suffering with me, and weeping with me. I can feel Him strengthening me in my weakness. Comforting me in my pain. Giving me peace in my anxiety and hope in my despair.

When you're hurting, don't grope in the darkness. Look for the Light of the world. Jesus wants to be a lamp for your feet and a light unto your path. A shining beacon of light at sunset that will lead you home to Him.

Lord Jesus, we thank You that You are with us in our suffering. When we're blinded by darkness, help us to see Your light leading us home to You. In Your precious name, amen.

I will lead the blind by ways they have not known, along unfamiliar paths I will guide them; I will turn the darkness into light before them and make the rough places smooth. These are the things I will do; I will not forsake them.
—ISAIAH 42:16

For Prayerful Reflection

How do you find the light of Jesus in the darkness?

_____

_____

_____

74

JESUS IS MY ETERNAL LIFE

In Me, there is no death.

—JESUS

*W*HEN YOU LOSE a loved one, you may feel lost and unable to cope. You may wonder how you can possibly go on. You may grieve, but you needn't despair. It's not the end for you—nor for your loved one who believes.

When Jesus heard from Mary and Martha that their brother Lazarus was sick, He risked His life to go to Jerusalem to heal His beloved friend. When He arrived, Lazarus was already dead. Jesus wept. But His tears were more for Mary and Martha than for the deceased. Why? Because Jesus knew what Mary and Martha didn't. Just as He overcame death, so do those who believe in Him. He would bring Lazarus back to life, just as He ushers all believers to eternal life.

You may miss the people in your life who have died. You may weep that you no longer have them by your side. But you can also rejoice. For just as Lazarus was raised from the dead, your loved ones who believed will also rise in Jesus. You will see them again in that far better place. Because, in Jesus, death is never the end.

Lord Jesus, we thank You that, just as You overcame death on a cross, You enable us to overcome death in You. We are so grateful that we can spend blessed eternity with You in heaven. To You be the glory forever and ever! In Your precious name, amen.

He will wipe every tear from their eyes. There will
be no more death or mourning or crying or pain,
for the old order of things has passed away.
—REVELATION 21:4

For Prayerful Reflection

How does knowing that believers never die help you cope with the loss of your loved ones?

_____

_____

_____

75

JESUS IS MY BEST DECISION

I will lead you according to My perfect will.

—JESUS

WHEN I HAVE an important decision to make, I wish I could send an e-mail to Jesus@heaven.com. Imagine what it would be like to receive the perfect solution in your inbox from Jesus Christ Himself! You can't e-mail Jesus. But you can look for the Lord's leadings in your life to help you make your best decisions.

I perceive the Lord's leading when someone comes into my life at just the right time, supplying just what I need to solve a perplexing problem. When an inner prompting directs me to a solution and continues to prompt me, even when I try to ignore it. When a Scripture verse comes to mind that suddenly takes on new meaning in light of my current dilemma. When I awaken early in the morning with a perfect answer that could only have come from the Lord.

You can't receive an email directly from the Lord. But isn't it reassuring to know that He never fails to find ways to lead you in the right direction?

Lord Jesus, we thank You for Your leadings in our lives. When we are faced with crucial decisions, help us to discern Your perfect will. And if we get it wrong, help us to trust in You to make it right. In Your precious name, amen.

Many are the plans in a person's heart, but
it is the LORD's purpose that prevails.
—PROVERBS 19:21

FOR PRAYERFUL REFLECTION

How do you perceive the Lord's leadings in your life?

_____

_____

_____

76

JESUS IS MY MASTER

Serve Me, and you will be blessed.

—JESUS

*W*HAT'S THE FIRST thing you'll ask Jesus when you get to heaven? I'd like to ask Him why there's so much suffering in the world. Why children go hungry. Why life can seem so unfair. Why I was struck down by a neuromuscular disease in the prime of my life. But I doubt I'll ask any of these questions. As I stand there, beholding my beloved Savior face-to-face, I'll probably have only one question in mind. I'll joyfully step forward with my new healthy legs, wipe tears of joy from my eyes, and humbly ask, "Lord, how can I best serve You?"

Serving Jesus is the greatest thing you do—both this side of heaven and on the other side. When you serve Jesus on Earth, the good you do reverberates in heaven. When you promote the Kingdom, you bring a little bit of heaven to Earth and make this world a far better place. Serve Jesus—and prepare to be amazed!

Lord Jesus, we thank You for the privilege of serving You. Enable us to be Your instruments on Earth and to serve You for all eternity. In Your precious name, amen.

The throne of God and of the Lamb will be in
the city, and his servants will serve him.
—REVELATION 22:3

For Prayerful Reflection

How are you blessed when you serve Jesus?

_____

_____

_____

77

JESUS IS MY TRANSFORMATION

I will change you to become more like Me.

—JESUS

*A*RE THERE THINGS about yourself that you want to change but don't know how? You're not alone. Thousands of people go to therapists every year because they want help to change. They may wish to increase their self-esteem, cope with depression, decrease anxiety, work on anger issues, improve their relationships. The list is long. Yet psychologists tell us that it's not easy to change. We have bad habits that are hard to break. Unhealthy thoughts that resist modification. Deep-seated emotions and issues that are difficult to uncover and treat. But you needn't despair.

God makes change possible in you. The Holy Spirit works in you every day, helping you to overcome sin and lead a righteous life. Enabling you to throw off your old self and put on your new self. Making you a new creation that is more like Christ.

When you're looking to change, look to the Lord. Pray to Him for discernment. He may or may not direct you to seek professional help. But He will always direct you to the Holy Spirit. Let the Spirit work in you—and watch how you begin to change in extraordinary ways!

Lord Jesus, we thank You that You make change possible in us. Help us to allow the Holy Spirit to work in us, so that we may become more like You every day. In Your precious name, amen.

You were taught, with regard to your former way of
life, to put off your old self, which is being corrupted
by its deceitful desires; to be made new in the attitude
of your minds; and to put on the new self, created to
be like God in true righteousness and holiness.
—EPHESIANS 4:22–24

FOR PRAYERFUL REFLECTION

In what ways is the Holy Spirit changing you?

_____

_____

_____

78

JESUS IS MY RIGHTEOUSNESS

In Me, you are justified.

—JESUS

*W*HEN YOU MESS up, do you imagine God saying, "There you go again!" You try to be good, resist temptation, keep your promises, be faithful, and obedient. But it's hard to stay on the straight and narrow. Somewhere along the way, you stray. You're not alone.

We're all fallen creatures who inevitably mess up, whether we want to or not. Even Paul admitted, "I do not understand what I do. For what I want to do I do not do, but what I hate I do" (Rom. 7:15). If Paul struggled with being good, how much hope is there for the rest of us? Not much, if our hope is in ourselves. But thankfully, our hope lies beyond ourselves.

When Jesus gave His life on the cross, He took away your sin so that you could be made sinless. Perfect and unblemished. Blameless before God. Justified and declared righteous through His saving sacrifice.

You can become more like the righteous person God sees when He sees you through Christ. How? By striving to become more like Jesus every day. It won't be easy. You may lose patience with yourself. But the Lord will never lose patience with you. You may think you're not worthy. But the Lord will never lose faith in you. You may think that you need to be born again— and again. But God knows that no matter how many times you stumble and fall. No matter how many old habits you return to, you need only return to Him. Praise God that, when we stray along the way, He always shows us the way!

Lord Jesus, we thank You that You sacrificed Yourself on the cross and took away our sin so that we could be made sinless, perfect, and unblemished in our Father's eyes. Help us to humbly pursue the righteousness You won for us by enabling us to become more like you every day. In Your precious name, amen.

Being confident of this, that he who began
a good work in you will carry it on to
completion until the day of Christ Jesus.
—PHILIPPIANS 1:6

FOR PRAYERFUL REFLECTION

What are you doing to become more like Christ?

_____

_____

_____

79

JESUS IS MY FOREVER PRESENCE

Look for Me with all your heart, and you will see Me.

—JESUS

$\mathcal{I}$T MAY BE hard to believe that God really shows up these days. It's not like it was in biblical times when God appeared in a burning bush, at Mount Sinai, and in Jesus Himself. What could be clearer than that? Yet, despite His coming to Earth in human form and performing healings and miracles, many still did not believe. Even after Jesus was crucified and appeared again, one of His own disciples was a doubting Thomas.

The good news is that, just as God showed up in history, He shows up today. In the beauty of nature. In His Word. In miracles. In inner promptings. In lives changed. You can see Him for yourself—if you know how to look.

Look for the Lord with all your heart. You'll feel His love when you're hurting. His hope when you despair. His saving grace when you feel that all is lost. The Lord is here today, filling heaven and Earth with His awesome presence. Can you see Him?

Lord Jesus, we thank You for showing up not just once, not just twice, but every minute of every day. Help us to behold Your presence, Your glory, and Your blessings in our lives. In Your precious name, amen.

~

"Am I only a God nearby," declares the LORD, "and not a God far away? Who can hide in secret places so that I cannot see them?" declares the LORD. "Do not I fill heaven and earth?" declares the LORD.
—JEREMIAH 23:23–24

FOR PRAYERFUL REFLECTION

In what ways does the Lord show up in your life?

_____

_____

_____

80

JESUS IS MY WAY THROUGH

I will make a way.

—JESUS

*I*T CAN BE upsetting when something unexpected happens. You're driving down the road, minding your own business, when suddenly you hit a roadblock. Maybe your house goes into foreclosure. Or you lose your job. Or your marriage breaks up. Or your health suddenly fails. They say that the best laid plans of mice and men often go astray. I don't know about the mice, but I can get pretty rattled when that happens. Especially when the roadblock is a progressive neuromuscular disease. Yet I've discovered something truly amazing.

When you're in Jesus, you needn't worry about unforeseen circumstances. Jesus has already foreseen your unforeseen circumstances. He will make a way through no matter what obstacles appear along the way. He will work all things for the good no matter how bad things seem. He will direct your steps and put you on a path that's even better than before!

Lord Jesus, we thank You that no matter what road-blocks we face, You always make a way through. Help us to reach out to You when we're stopped in our tracks. So that You can put us on the right path. In Your precious name, amen.

In their hearts humans plan their course, but
the LORD establishes their steps.
—PROVERBS 16:9

For Prayerful Reflection

How does Jesus help you get through unforeseen circumstances?

_____

_____

_____

81

JESUS IS MY PROMISE

You can rely on My promises.

—**JESUS**

*W*HEN TROUBLES PERSIST, many of us have difficulty maintaining faith. We may believe God has forsaken us. We may fear that He's not listening and doesn't care. How can you maintain faith in the face of cruel reality? Don't rely on your own understanding —but on God's promises.

God promises to give you hope and a future (Jer. 29:11). He promises that He will make you strong and steadfast (1 Pet. 5:10). He promises that He "will make your paths straight" (Prov. 3:6). He promises that He will work all things for the good for those who love him (Rom. 8:28). He promises that He "will be with you wherever you go" (Joshua 1:9). Perhaps the greatest promise of all is God's promise of eternal life (John 3:16). These are just some of the thousands of promises in the Bible!

Corrie ten Boom wrote, "Let God's promises shine on your problems."[1] When it's hard to hang onto faith, remember that God is faithful. He always keeps His promises. On that you can rely—both on Earth and in heaven!

Lord Jesus, we thank You that You are faithful. Help us not to rely on our own understanding but on Your amazing promises. Enable us to remember that, no matter how hopeless our lives seem, You always come through for us. In Your precious name, amen.

മ

And this is what he promised us—eternal life.
—1 JOHN 2:25

FOR PRAYERFUL REFLECTION

How do God's promises help you get through hard times?

_____

_____

_____

82

JESUS IS MY PATIENCE

Wait upon Me. I'll give you exactly what you need.

—JESUS

*W*HEN YOU'RE GOING through difficult times and waiting for the Lord to rescue you, it's hard to be patient. God promises, "I am with you….I will strengthen you and help you; I will uphold you with my righteous right hand" (Isa. 41:10). But it's not easy to hold onto His promises when you're holding on for dear life. When you're anxiously waiting for God to answer your prayers, what can you do?

Ask the Lord to give you patience. Wait with optimism not pessimism. Hope not despair. Praise not complaint. Prayer not silence. Trust in Him. Have faith that He is working things out for the good and will answer you in a big way. Giving you exactly what you need in His perfect timing.

Wait patiently upon the Lord. Hold on tight to Him—and His promises—and your patience will be richly rewarded.

Lord Jesus, we thank You that You answer our prayers with exactly what we need. Help us to be patient as You work in our lives to bring about good. In Your precious name, amen.

Be joyful in hope, patient in affliction, faithful in prayer.
—ROMANS 12:12

FOR PRAYERFUL REFLECTION

How do you find patience as you wait for the Lord to act in your life?

_____

_____

_____

83

JESUS IS MY POSITIVITY

I help you to overcome bad with good.

—JESUS

*S*OMETIMES LIFE CAN feel like a moon mission gone wrong. You're flying high until something catastrophic threatens your plans. At times like these, it's easy to focus on the bad. But what if you ask yourself, "What do I have that's good?"

That's what Gene Kranz, NASA flight director, thought as the Apollo 13 crew hurtled toward the moon, facing death. Thousands of miles above the earth, one of the oxygen tanks had exploded. The calamity not only threatened to derail the moon mission, but also jeopardized the lives of the astronauts. Kranz utilized everything that was good on the ship to bring the astronauts safely back to Earth.[1] In doing so, he was taking a page right out of the Bible. Scripture tells us: "Whatever is true, whatever is noble, whatever is right, whatever is pure, whatever is lovely, whatever is admirable—if anything is excellent or praiseworthy—think about such things... And the God of peace will be with you" (Phil. 4:8–9). Why does the Lord want you to be positive?

Positivity can enhance your life by reducing stress and increasing your health and longevity. It can lead to a better marriage and more friends. Most importantly, when negativity is brought on by dark forces that threaten to turn you away from the Lord, positivity can open your heart and bring you back to Him.

When you're feeling negative, summon the positivity to call upon Jesus. He'll help you to utilize the good in your life to overcome the bad. He'll keep your ship afloat and bring you in for a safe landing.

Lord Jesus, we thank You that You create the positive in our lives. Help us to overcome bad with good. Enable us to combat negativity by remaining positive in You. In Your precious name, amen.

I am making a way in the wilderness
and streams in the wasteland.
—Isaiah 43:19

For Prayerful Reflection

How does the Lord make a way for you to overcome bad with good in your life?

_____

_____

_____

84

JESUS IS MY CAPACITY TO LOVE

Love Me and love others as yourself.

—JESUS

*A*RE YOU FEARFUL of forming new relationships? Love is a great blessing, but it can also have a downside. A loving relationship gone wrong can cause you to feel vulnerable, let down, rejected, and betrayed. No one knew this better than Jesus. Despite loving His disciples unconditionally, He was denied by Peter three times, doubted by Thomas, and betrayed by Judas. Despite showering everyone He met with love, He was crucified by the very people He came to Earth to save.

Yet Jesus commands you to love—not just Him but also others. Why? Because He is the very embodiment of love. His love is the most powerful force in the universe! When He shines His love through you to others, hearts turn, lives are transformed, and the world changes for the better.

Don't be afraid to love. You can rest assured that, even if others let you down, Jesus never will. He will comfort your broken heart, and help you to find the courage to love again.

Lord Jesus, we thank You for loving us. Enable us to love You with all our heart, all our soul, all our mind, and all our strength. Help us to love our neighbors as ourselves. In Your precious name, amen.

ॐ

"The most important one," answered Jesus, "is this: 'Hear, O Israel: The Lord our God, the Lord is one. Love the Lord your God with all your heart and with all your soul and with all your mind and with all your strength.' The second is this: 'Love your neighbor as yourself.' There is no commandment greater than these."

—MARK 12:29–31

FOR PRAYERFUL REFLECTION

How does Jesus's love for you enable you to love Him and others?

_____

_____

_____

85

JESUS IS MY SAFETY BELT

I will never let go of you.

—**Jesus**

*L*IFE CAN FEEL like you're riding a runaway roller-coaster. One minute things are fine. The next minute you're in free fall. One minute you're living the good life. The next minute you're holding on for dear life. Life is like that—full of highs and lows, and ups and downs.

My life is no exception. It's like the proverbial box of chocolates—I never know what I'm going to get! One day I feel a little stronger. The next day I'm weak again. One day I have intense pain. The next day it subsides a little. On bad days I'm tempted to worry about the "what ifs." What if I'm in a permanent downturn? What if I don't recover my functioning? In those moments I feel like I'm on a roller coaster, plunging two hundred feet fast. Holding on so tight that my knuckles turn white. That's when I remind myself to just let go—and let God.

When you're in Jesus, you don't have to "white knuckle" it. He is your safety belt. Let go of fear and hold on tight to the Lord. Let go of despair and hold on tight to His promises. Let go of anxiety and hold on tight to trust. Let go of worry and hold on tight to prayer. When you feel like you're in free fall, don't be afraid to let go—and let God. He will never let go of you.

Lord Jesus, we thank You that, when we're in the midst of turmoil, You are there with us, holding us in Your grasp. Help us to hold on tight to You and to never let go. In Your precious name, amen.

꩜

Cast your cares on the LORD and he will sustain
you; he will never let the righteous be shaken.
—PSALM 55:22

FOR PRAYERFUL REFLECTION

When have you let go—and let God?

_____

_____

_____

86

JESUS IS MY SPIRITUAL TRAINER

Grow spiritually in Me.

—JESUS

OULDN'T IT BE nice if life could be one long spring break? You may wish to live a life of leisure. But Jesus loves you too much to sell you short. He knows the benefits of your going through trials. He also knows the blessings that you may not recognize until you get to heaven.

Overcoming challenges can help you become spiritually fit. To grow and mature. To learn to be faithful, obedient, humble, trusting, loving, and persevering. To become a well-tuned instrument to serve the Lord. Life on Earth may not be one long spring break. But it's a gymnasium for the soul. And Jesus is your spiritual trainer—preparing you for all eternity.

When you meet Jesus in heaven, how would you like to show up? Spiritually fit or spiritually flabby? With your old shabby self or renewed in the image of Christ? When you persevere in the Lord, you may not win any medals on Earth. But think of all the crowns you'll receive in heaven!

Lord Jesus, we thank You that You provide us with a gymnasium for the soul to prepare us for eternal life with You. Help us to persevere through our many trials and become spiritually fit. So that when we stand before You in heaven, we will hear You call us Your good and faithful servants. In Your precious name, amen.

Consider it pure joy, my brothers and sisters, whenever
you face trials of many kinds, because you know
that the testing of your faith produces perseverance.
Let perseverance finish its work so that you may be
mature and complete, not lacking anything.
—James 1:2–4

For Prayerful Reflection

What are you doing to become spiritually fit?

_____

_____

_____

87

JESUS IS MY REASSURANCE

I will take your burdens upon Myself.

—JESUS

*W*E ALL HAVE sleepless nights worrying about one thing or another. I recently heard a joke about a guy named Jack. He was such a compulsive worrier that he decided to hire a man named Tom to worry for him. When his friend Bob asked him how much it cost to hire a professional worrier, Jack replied, "Five thousand dollars per month." Bob exclaimed, "That's outrageous. How on Earth can you afford it? You must be up all night worrying." Jack replied. "No, I'm not. That's what I pay Tom for!"[1] Thankfully Jesus gives you a much better and less expensive alternative—Himself.

Jesus doesn't want you to be anxious about anything. Put your worries aside and place yourself in His hands. He'll take your burdens upon Himself. He'll give you the peace that transcends all understanding. He'll put an end to your worrying—and He won't even charge you for it!

Lord Jesus, we thank You that You take our burdens upon Yourself. Help us to reach out to You when we're worrying so that we may experience Your blessed peace. In Your precious name, amen.

Are not two sparrows sold for a penny? Yet not one of them will fall to the ground outside your Father's care.
—MATTHEW 10:29

FOR PRAYERFUL REFLECTION

In what ways does Jesus help you overcome your worrying?

_____

_____

_____

88

JESUS IS MY LIFE MAP

I will direct your steps.

—JESUS

*I*T'S NOT ALWAYS easy to admit that we're lost or going the wrong way in life. We'd rather wing it, take the next turn, and hope for the best rather than ask for directions. Unfortunately, this usually makes things worse.

When you're wandering without direction in life, stop and ask for directions. Not from just anyone. But from Someone who not only holds the map for your life, but also designed it. Jesus knows where you should begin, because He's been with you from the very beginning. He knows where you're going, because He sees your destination. When you can't find your way, find Jesus. He'll not only point you in the right direction and direct your steps. He'll also lovingly lead you to where you're destined to be.

Lord Jesus, we thank You that You not only know the way—You also are the way. Help us to not go it alone but to admit that we need Your help. Enable us to stop and ask You for directions. In Your precious name, amen.

The steps of a man are established by the LORD, when he delights in his way.
—PSALM 37:23, ESV

FOR PRAYERFUL REFLECTION

In what ways does Jesus direct your steps?

_____

_____

_____

89

JESUS IS MY BEST SELF

The good in you comes from Me.

—JESUS

*W*HETHER WE'RE YOUNG or old, sick or well, we wish that our time on Earth were longer. But we're like daylilies that brilliantly bloom for only a day, spending but a brief time in the sun. We're here one minute and gone the next. The Bible tells us, "They spring up like flowers and wither away; like fleeting shadows, they do not endure" (Job 14:2). Measured in days, our lifespan is but a wink of an eye in the great expanse of time. Yet it's not how we measure our days that matters—but how we spend them.

Despite your best intentions, you may not always spend your time wisely. We're all fallen creatures who are far from good and don't always make the best choices. Thankfully, the good in you comes not from yourself but from the Lord. He's the love in you that enables you to love others. The grace in you that enables you to be gracious to others. The mercy in you that enables you to be merciful to others. The forgiveness in you that enables you to forgive others. The servant in you that enables you to serve others.

While you're here, make the most of your time. Let God's goodness in you flow to others. You'll not only be making their lives better and this world a far better place. You'll also be making yourself a better person—becoming your very best self in Jesus.

Lord Jesus, we thank You that You are the good in us. Help us to be our very best selves in You. Allow Your goodness to flow through us to others. May our good works on Earth reverberate in heaven! In Your precious name, amen.

_ϡℓ_

I have been crucified with Christ and I no
longer live, but Christ lives in me.
—GALATIANS 2:20

FOR PRAYERFUL REFLECTION

What can you do to be your best self in Jesus?

_____

_____

_____

90

JESUS IS MY BEST LIFE

I can give you what no one else can in life.

—JESUS

*N*OWADAYS, PEOPLE ARE striving to live "the good life." To have the best house, the best car, the best job, and the best health. Once upon a time, I had it all. Until I was stricken with a neuromuscular disease and lost it all. I thought my life was over. I thought I couldn't go on. That's when I met Jesus and discovered that what I lost didn't compare to what I found. Even when you have the best that life can offer, it's not nearly as good as what the Lord can offer you.

Jesus gives you what you can't find anywhere else. He showers you with unmerited grace and unconditional love. He takes away your sins and forgives you. He grants you a peace that transcends all understanding. He creates a blessed, eternal relationship with you. He even transforms you into a new you, conformed to His very image. If you want to live your best life, spend your life in Jesus. There's nothing better than that!

Lord Jesus, we thank You that You give us what nothing else on Earth can. Help us to live our best lives in You each and every day. In Your precious name, amen.

I have come that they may have life, and have it to the full.

--JOHN 10:10

FOR PRAYERFUL REFLECTION

How does Jesus make your life your best life?

_____

_____

_____

IN GRATITUDE

*M*Y DEEP DEVOTION to Jesus led me to write this book. But Jesus made it happen. He lifted me out of my sick bed. He strengthened me when I was too weak to write. He gave me clarity of mind when I was too exhausted to think. He gifted me with vision to see Him through the blur of my suffering. He gave me hope and reassurance when I despaired. He gave me perseverance to overcome overwhelming challenges. That this book has come to completion is a testament to His amazing love and grace.

The Lord also worked though His body of believers in powerful ways. I'd like to express my gratitude to the many people who graciously supported me through the writing of this book.

Reverend David Stewart—the "pastor of hearts," as I fondly call him—has been a long-time cherished friend. He never fails to lift my spirits, brightening my days with his humor, challenging my mind with his spiritual insights, and gladdening my soul with his steadfast faith. He recently introduced me to the members of his congregation at the Dighton Community Church, who gave generously to my ministry. When I find myself looking for someone with the heart of Jesus, I look no further than Dave's amazing heart.

Dave, who brings such good things into my life, introduced me to Nancy W. Johnson. Nancy took me into her loving heart in a very special way. She has become a cherished friend and a true blessing in my life. I'm so thankful for her enthusiastic support, wise guidance, and constant prayer. She is truly a gift from God. I'm grateful to her and for her.

The miraculous events surrounding the writing and publication of this devotional could only have been brought about by the power and grace of Jesus Christ. To Him be the glory forever and ever! May this book honor Him by shining His light and love into the hearts of all those who journey through these pages. May it bring them hope and comfort, and strengthen their walk with Jesus day by day.

Our journey together need not end here. You can always find me on my website at www.docbeverlyrose.com. My Facebook page is at www.facebook.com/DrBeverlyRose. It's a daily Christian ministry of hope and healing. Come join our wonderful community of believers. We gather daily to support, encourage, and inspire each other in our walk with the Lord. We'd love to meet you!

~Joe~

Just as God's love and mercies are new every morning, so are your opportunities. To renew your love for the Lord. To strengthen your commitment to Him. To walk more closely with Him. To love others as yourself. To allow His Spirit to lead you in new and marvelous ways to do great things. Jesus is reaching out to you. Will you take His hand and make Him *your* Jesus?

NOTES

Introduction

1. Adapted from *Mothers Never Die* by Beverly Rose (Nashville, TN: Thomas Nelson, 2002). Used by permission.

9—Jesus Is My Vision

1. Heien Keller, "Helen Keller Quotes," HelenKellerOnline.com, http://www.helenkelleronline.com/#quotes (accessed February 2, 2016).

10—Jesus Is My Reason for Being

1. Sue Shanahan, "Over the Rainbow: Your Life's Purpose," *Huffington Post* online, May 26, 2015, http://www.huffingtonpost.com/sue -shanahan/over-the-rainbow-your-lif_b_5034854.html (accessed February 1, 2016).

31—Jesus Is My Enlightenment

1. Art Lindsley, "C. S. Lewis' Seven Key Ideas," C. S. Lewis Institute, http://www.cslewisinstitute.org/node/44 (accessed February 3, 2016).

39—Jesus Is My All-Weather Friend

1. Corrie ten Boom, "Cornelia 'Corrie' ten Boom," Missionaries Biography.com, http://www.missionariesbiography.com/April/15.Cornelia _ten_Boom.html (accessed February 3, 2015).

44—Jesus Is My "All-In"

1. Elisabeth Elliot, *Through Gates of Splendor* (Carol Stream, IL: Tyndale Momentum, 1981), 8.

53—Jesus Is My Cushion

1. Tim Thurman, "Relying on God Has to Begin All Over Again Every Day...," *The Wisdom of C. S. Lewis* (blog), June 26, 2011, http:// cslewiswisdom.blogspot.com/2011/06/relying-on-god-has-to-begin-all -over.html (accessed March 7, 2016).

66—Jesus Is My Grace

1. Max Lucado, *Great Day, Every Day* (Nashville, TN: Thomas Nelson, 2012), 24.

69—Jesus Is My Destination

1. Charles Stanley, *A Touch of His Freedom* (Grand Rapids, MI: Zondervan, 2012), 45.

81—JESUS IS MY PROMISE

1. Debbie McDaniel, "40 Powerful Quotes From Corrie ten Boom," Crosswalk.com, May 21, 2015, http://www.crosswalk.com/faith /women/40-powerful-quotes-from-corrie-ten-boom.html (accessed February 4, 2016).

83—JESUS IS MY POSITIVITY

1. Carol D. Bos, JD, "Apollo 13—Gene Kranz at Mission Control," AwesomeStories.com, October 7, 2013, https://www.awesomestories.com /asset/view/Apollo-13-Gene-Kranz-at-Mission-Control (accessed March 7, 2016).

87—JESUS IS MY REASSURANCE

1. "Worry-wart," BestCleanJokes.com, http://www.bestcleanjokes.com /Worry-wart.htm (accessed March 7, 2016).

ABOUT THE AUTHOR

*D*R. BEVERLY ROSE is an ordained minister who has a doctor of ministry degree in Christian counseling. She is also a clinical psychologist with a doctor of psychology degree. She received postdoctoral training at Harvard Medical School, where she subsequently held an academic appointment as instructor in psychology. She is the author of *Mothers Never Die* (Thomas Nelson) and *So Close, I Can Feel God's Breath* (Tyndale House). Dr. Rose has appeared nationally on radio and television, inspiring thousands of people with her story. Despite her daily trials of living with a neuromuscular disease, she experiences great joy and hope in her walk with the Lord.